100
BEST
FOODS FOR
PREGNANCY

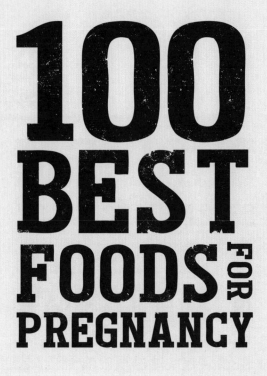

100 BEST FOODS FOR PREGNANCY

Charlotte Watts

This edition published by Parragon Books Ltd in 2015 and distributed by

Parragon Inc.
440 Park Avenue South, 13th Floor
New York, NY 10016
www.parragon.com/lovefood

LOVE FOOD is an imprint of Parragon Books Ltd

ISBN 978-1-4748-1227-6

Printed in China

Created and produced by Ivy Contract
New photography by Clive Streeter
Additional recipes by Nicola Graimes

Notes for the Reader
This book uses standard kitchen measuring spoons and cups. All spoon and cup measurements are level unless otherwise indicated. Unless otherwise stated, milk is assumed to be whole, eggs are large, individual vegetables are medium, pepper is freshly ground black pepper, and salt is table salt. Unless otherwise stated, all root vegetables should be peeled prior to using.

For best results, use a food thermometer when cooking meat. Check the latest government guidelines for current advice.

Cover photograph by Max and Liz Haarala Hamilton

CONTENTS

INTRODUCTION

When you are pregnant, your body requires more vitamins, minerals, and essential fatty acids right from the moment of conception. In this book, we will guide you through the foods and diet that will best help you achieve the healthiest pregnancy for the well-being of both you and your baby.

Good nutrition can help you to remain completely active during pregnancy and keep up your energy levels so that you can look after your newborn and recover more quickly after the birth. This means preparing as much food as possible yourself from fresh, whole ingredients instead of relying on processed food. It is important to follow current government guidance on food, drinks, and activity for a healthy pregnancy. No single food has any special nutrients or powers that can change the overall health of individuals; it is the combination of food, drinks, and lifestyle, and making balanced choices, that can provide the nutrients and energy your body needs for a healthy pregnancy.

Weight before, during, and after pregnancy

Addressing weight issues needs to happen before conception. This includes gaining weight if you are under your ideal weight to support production of the hormones you need to conceive. If you are overweight, talk to your doctor or health-care provider about your ideal

weight to help increase your fertility and lessen the risk of pregnancy complications, such as diabetes and high blood pressure. Weight loss is not advised during pregnancy.

Normal weight gain during pregnancy is between 25–35 pounds, but it will depend on your build and height. On average, this is ¾–1 pound per week after the first trimester. Even though your heart rate and nutrient needs increase during pregnancy, you don't have to consume more calories until the third trimester, when your requirements go up by about 10 percent. Morning sickness can cause weight loss, so building up your appetite to regain weight when it passes is crucial.

Until at least six weeks after birth, focus on eating healthily instead of losing weight. Weight loss will occur naturally and safely without hindering your recovery if you concentrate on eating regular meals and avoid relying on convenience foods wherever possible.

General dietary guidelines

A mother's diet needs to supply all of the energy and nutritional needs of the developing fetus, as well as her own, so a consistent, healthy, and varied diet is essential:

* Eat regular meals and never skip breakfast—you need regular energy and your baby needs a constant fuel supply for optimum growth and development. Breakfast keeps these levels sustained throughout the day, lessens cravings for unhealthy foods later, and helps you avoid "highs and lows" of energy and mood.
* Snack healthily—especially if your appetite is lowered, or your growing belly means you eat less at meals because there is less room in your stomach. Even if you feel nauseous or lacking in appetite, try to eat something healthy at least every four hours. The occasional treat is fine.
* Aim to eat more in the lead up to the birth—you will need the energy stores both for labor and for recovery afterward. This may need to be little and often as your growing baby will probably put pressure on your digestive system.
* Stay hydrated—from conception to breast-feeding, your body needs fluids to help eliminate harmful toxins, support the immunity of mother and baby, and maintain the growth of the fetus.

Specific nutritional considerations

Extra protein—your needs increase by up to a third during pregnancy because it is used to build your baby's body. Lean meat, certain fish (see pages 10–11 for more information), eggs (thoroughly cooked), pasteurized dairy produce, and vegetable proteins (tofu, beans, nuts, seeds, and dried beans) are good sources. Protein should be included in every meal.

Healthy oils and fats are required constantly—fertility, pregnancy hormones, your recovery after birth, and your baby's organs (such as heart, liver, and brain) rely on their daily intake. Oily fish, such as salmon (wild or organic), mackerel (not king mackerel), herring, sardines, fresh anchovies, trout, and pilchards, provide omega-3 fatty acids and are safe to consume while pregnant; however, do not eat more than 12 ounces a week. Do not take cod liver oil supplements when pregnant—they contain very high levels of vitamin A, which may lead to birth defects. Vegetarian foods, such as green leafy vegetables, and moderate amounts of nuts and seeds, provide omega-3 and omega-6 fatty acids. Healthy monounsaturated fats are found in avocados, walnuts, and olive oil.

Complex carbohydrates—these are rich in fiber, B vitamins, folic acid (folate), iron, and magnesium, which all support pregnancy. They are also particularly good for easing constipation, a common pregnancy problem. A diet rich in beans, legumes, whole grains, and vegetables will provide these constant energy sources.

Iron intake is important during pregnancy because your body makes extra red blood cells. Iron-rich proteins are particularly beneficial (meat, beans, eggs, and tofu). Green leafy vegetables provide both iron and vitamin C, the latter needed for iron's absorption. Vegetarians and vegans will need to have their iron levels monitored by their doctor and may require a supplement.

Calcium intake must be kept up during pregnancy and if breast-feeding, to support the formation and growth of your baby's skeleton. As well as dairy produce, green leafy vegetables, nuts, and seeds are good sources of this mineral. These also provide magnesium, which is needed for bone development.

Fruit and vegetables are rich in immune-supporting antioxidants, such as vitamins C, E, and zinc. Different colors provide different benefits and so variety is essential. Consuming at least five portions a day—two servings of fruit and at least three of vegetables—may help to support a mother's immunity and provides a good supply of vitamin C, needed for healthy bones, skin, and collagen production.

Using this book

Many of the foods in this book are healthy during every stage of pregnancy. However, some are included for specific reasons at a particular stage and may have contraindications at another—for example, foods that promote breast milk flow are not advised during pregnancy. Read each entry and build up a varied and tasty diet from the foods available to you before including. Any herbs mentioned in this book should be eaten only in normal culinary use and avoided in larger

medicinal amounts. Discuss any changes in your diet with your doctor or health-care provider. There is a comprehensive table of specific foods to avoid during pregnancy on pages 10–11.

Key to recipe codes
Recipes within the book are accompanied by the following codes:

(**G**) Growth of baby—contains nutrients that particularly support full and healthy growth of your baby's body.

(**B**) Brain development of baby—particularly supportive of constant growth of brain cells and future cognitive function of your baby.

(**A**) Immunity-supporting antioxidants—substances that help prevent infection, inflammation, and tissue damage that can affect fertility, pregnancy, and recovery.

(**N**) Natural remedy—has specific properties shown to help relieve common pregnancy and post-pregnancy symptoms, often with a long history of traditional use.

(**V**) Suitable for vegetarians.

(**Q**) Quick and easy to prepare.

Foods to avoid or reduce while pregnant

Certain foods must be avoided during pregnancy to reduce the risk of harm to both mother and baby—for a full list, consult the chart on pages 10–11. Official advice on what is safe to eat during pregnancy can change, so always consult your health-care provider for the latest information.

There are a number of foods that are inherently deemed "unhealthy" and offer high calories with little nutritional value, known as "empty calories." They are usually processed, refined, and high in sugar, salt, and unhealthy fats; they are often fried or the fats are damaged in the cooking process. These present a risk in pregnancy not just because of their lack of supportive nutrients, but also because they may reduce the body's immune, circulatory, and detoxification ability. They may also contribute to cell damage and increase your need for more protective antioxidant nutrients, such as vitamins C and E. Note that convenience foods and prepared meals tend to be high in salt, unhealthy fats, and chemical additives, so are best avoided during pregnancy.

Refined foods, such as sugar, white flour, and white rice are termed "simple carbohydrates" and provide little nutritional value or fiber. They are quickly digested, causing sudden rises in blood sugar that may lead to low energy and the loss of vital pregnancy nutrients. Foods with high fat and refined sugars, such as pastries, cakes, and cookies, are the most unhealthy.

Hydrogenated vegetable oils found in margarines may interfere with the body's utilization of essential fatty acids. Check food labels—foods containing hydrogenated fats are usually highly processed and may contain other undesirable chemical additives.

Burned fats are known to be harmful to the body because they contain high levels of free radicals, which can damage cells and tissues. Avoid overcooked meats and charred, grilled food.

Note that it is now considered safe to eat foods containing peanuts during pregnancy unless there is a family history of allergy or your health-care provider advises you not to.

A word on colic, reflux, and gas in breast-fed babies

There is much discussion on which foods may or may not cause digestive issues in breast-fed babies, and many cultures differ in opinion. Although evidence suggests that the factors that cause gas in the mother do not actually reach breast milk, individual mothers cite different foods that they observe affecting their babies. Consider foods that you may not tolerate as potential problems, and monitor your baby after you eat different foods. Bear in mind that colic, reflux, and gas problems are an issue of the baby's underdeveloped digestion, and time is the best healer.

Specific pregnancy risk factors

Risk factor/risk	Foods/substances to avoid
Listeria infection Rare, but can cause flulike illness linked to miscarriage, stillbirth, or severe illness in newborn babies	• All types of pâté, even vegetarian • Soft, blue-vein, and Mexican-style cheeses • Prepared meals; insufficiently reheated food
Salmonella infection Food poisoning will not directly harm the baby but may make the mother very unwell	• Raw meat, poultry, and fish • Unpasteurized milk • Raw eggs and raw egg products
Campylobacter infection Bacterial infection linked to miscarriage and premature labor	• As for salmonella—see above • Untreated water
Toxoplasmosis infection Rare, but infection can lead to serious problems for the baby	• Raw or undercooked meat • Cured meat, such as salami and Parma ham • Soil; cat feces
Dioxins and PCBs Harmful pollutants, such as dioxins, PCBs, and methyl mercury, can be found in fish and shellfish	• Avoid shark, swordfish, tilefish, king mackerel—all high in mercury. Limit intake of fish/shellfish that are lower in mercury to 12 oz a week (2 meals)
Xenoestrogen exposure Hormone disruptor that may interfere with pregnancy hormones	• Soft plastics; pesticides, herbicides, and fertilizers; meat and dairy containing growth hormones
High concentrations of vitamin A High intake in pregnancy has been linked to a higher than average risk of birth defects	• Liver, or liver-containing products, such as pâté • Cod liver oil • Multivitamin supplements containing vitamin A
Parasitic infection, such as tapeworm Digestive problems can lead to severe food poisoning	• Undercooked or raw shellfish
Caffeine A stimulant that in large amounts may deplete calcium and raise blood pressure; possible link to miscarriage in high doses	• Tea and coffee • Sodas, energy drinks, and chocolate • Some medications
Alcohol Intake has been linked to a reduction in birth weight, and also birth defects and miscarriage	• All wines, beers, and liquors
Salt Added to food and in processed foods can contribute to high blood pressure	• Added table salt • Processed and convenience foods
Herbs Outside of normal culinary use, herbs in large doses can interfere with pregnancy hormones	• Large amounts of herbal teas • Herbal supplements

Alternatives/action

- Hummus and guacamole make good alternatives
- Eat hard cheeses, such as cheddar
- Be sure food is cooked all the way through and reheated properly

- Check raw meat and fish is stored safely and cooked thoroughly; wash hands after preparing. Avoid sashimi
- Check labels; most dairy is now pasteurized, but unpasteurized products may be sold at farmers' markets
- Only eat eggs cooked until white and yolk are solid; avoid homemade mayonnaise/mousse with raw eggs

- As for salmonella—see above
- Drink clean water and bottled water if sources are unsure

- Check meat is cooked thoroughly
- Choose uncured cold meats, such as turkey or chicken slices
- Wash all fruit and vegetables; do not handle litter trays

- Commonly eaten fish that are lower in mercury include shrimp, salmon, pollock, catfish, and canned light tuna. Albacore (white) tuna has more mercury than light tuna, so keep to one 6 oz serving per week. All the fish contained in this book is safe to eat

- Avoid storing fatty foods in soft plastics (such as plastic wrap); avoid microwaving foods in plastic—transfer foods to glass containers or cook conventionally. Wash fruit and vegetables before eating. Consider buying organic meat, dairy, and eggs where possible

- Choose alternative protein sources, such as turkey or beef. Avoid all pâtés
- Omega-3 fatty acid supplements designed for use during pregnancy—check with your health-care provider
- Prenatal supplements that contain vitamin A in the form of beta-carotene are safe to consume

- Ensure all shellfish is cooked thoroughly

- Wean off tea and coffee to just one or two cups a day with food; avoid, if possible
- Avoid sodas and energy drinks, and limit chocolate to a treat
- Check with your health-care provider

- Safe limits are inconclusive, so best to avoid

- Celery salt or spices

- Vary herbal teas and limit to one or two cups a day (see our guidelines for entries in this book)
- Avoid all herbal supplements in pregnancy and while breast-feeding
- Check with your doctor or a dietitian for herbs used for fertility

Fertility and Conception

In the preparation stage before pregnancy, the nutritional focus is on increasing the nutrients needed for egg and sperm health and reducing the factors that may harm these. Vitamins A and C and other antioxidants can help protect the egg and sperm from damage by chemicals and pollutants. Low levels of zinc may affect fertility in both men and women, while folic acid levels have to be high to help prevent birth defects. Good dietary protein levels are also required for conception.

In this chapter, we focus on foods that provide dense nutritional content relevant to conception support, and that offer an alternative to foods that may affect fertility. Guidelines also support weight loss before pregnancy, which is the safe time for any excess to be lost.

(G) Growth of baby

(B) Brain development of baby

(A) Immunity-supporting antioxidants

(N) Natural remedy

(V) Suitable for vegetarians

(Q) Quick and easy to prepare

01

PUMPKIN SEEDS

Seeds, which encapsulate all that is necessary for the beginnings of plant life, contain high levels of the nutrients needed for fertility.

MAJOR NUTRIENTS PER 15 G/ABOUT 2 TBSP PUMPKIN SEEDS

Calories	81
Total fat	6.9 g
Monounsaturated fat	2.44 g
Omega-6 fatty acids	3,105 mg
Omega-9 fatty acids	2,122 mg
Protein	4.53 g
Carbohydrate	1.61 g
Fiber	0.9 g
Vitamin B1	0.04 mg
Vitamin B3	0.75 mg
Vitamin B5	0.11 mg
Vitamin E	1.64 mg
Magnesium	88.8 mg
Potassium	121.4 mg
Phosphorus	184.95 mg
Iron	1.32 mg
Manganese	0.68 mg
Selenium	1.41 mcg
Zinc	1.17 mg

Pumpkin seeds contain particularly high levels of zinc, which is needed for all aspects of reproductive health, including healthy hormones and eggs, and creating new cells for growth. These precious seeds are also an excellent source of vitamin E, the most important antioxidant when it comes to protecting eggs from damage. Vitamin E works together with the selenium content to help create a healthy womb lining, ready for fertilization and implantation. Pumpkin seeds are also one of the best plant sources of omega-3 fatty acids, and deliver these in good balance with omega-6 fatty acids—in combination, these two play a vital role in keeping the oily outer layer of an egg intact.

- Contain zinc, which is essential for reproduction.
- Vitamin E content and high levels of essential fatty acids keep eggs healthy and primed for fertilization.
- Contain vitamin E and selenium in an effective combination to ensure the optimum womb environment for conception.

Practical tips:
Store pumpkin seeds in airtight jars away from heat and light in order to keep the easily perishable essential fatty acids and vitamin E from damage that can affect their potency. Eat these seeds as healthy snacks in place of sugary foods that may reduce fertility. Add to salads to provide extra protein and healthy fat content.

Couscous, chickpea, and pumpkin seed pilaf

SERVES 4   (G) (A) (V) (Q)

1 cup barley couscous

1½ cups vegetable stock

1 large yellow bell pepper,
*   seeded and chopped*

4 scallions, chopped

10 plumped dried apricots,
*   chopped*

⅓ cup golden raisins

½ cup slivered almonds

⅓ cup walnut pieces

1 tbsp pumpkin seeds

5½ oz of canned chickpeas
*   (garbanzo beans), drained*
*   and rinsed (⅔ cup)*

2 tbsp pumpkin seed oil

Method

1 Put the couscous in a large, heatproof bowl. Heat the stock in a saucepan to boiling point, then pour over the couscous and stir well. Cover and let stand for 15 minutes, by which time all the liquid should have been absorbed.

2 Stir all the remaining ingredients, except the oil, into the couscous, forking through lightly. Serve drizzled with the oil.

02

LEMONS

Lemon is an extremely useful and versatile ingredient. It will increase the cleansing and detoxifying actions of the body that are so important for conception.

Lemons are very high in vitamin C, a major antioxidant that helps protect eggs and the uterine wall—as well as sperm—from damage from toxins. Their cleansing effect is heightened by their alkalizing action inside the body. Although they taste very acidic, once eaten, lemons actually help to balance our acid–alkaline levels. This balance is crucial in women for their hormones to work efficiently and to ensure a hospitable environment for sperm. In men, it lets the body store sperm safely. The high potassium level in lemons also ensures that fluid reaches the cells, keeping the body hydrated, and helps to maintain healthy mucous levels within the female reproductive organs, which enables egg implantation.

- Very high in vitamin C, which protects the egg and womb from pollutants that can interfere with fertilization.
- Keep the body in an alkaline state, so promoting optimum hormone function and hydration.
- Keep digestion efficient so that you get the most nutrients possible from your diet.

Practical tips:
Lemon juice is an excellent flavoring in dressings. Use in place of vinegars because these may exacerbate yeast and digestive problems. Lemon juice also tastes great with water, in place of a sugary beverage. For the most cleansing effect, make the water hot and add the juice of up to half a lemon.

DID YOU KNOW?

In traditional Chinese medicine, lemon water has been prescribed to boost fertility for centuries. It is believed to increase hydration, while also flushing out toxins from the body.

MAJOR NUTRIENTS PER MEDIUM-SIZE LEMON

Calories	17
Total fat	0.17 g
Protein	0.64 g
Carbohydrate	5.41 g
Fiber	1.6 g
Vitamin C	30.7 mg
Potassium	80 mg

Chickpea soup with a Moroccan sauce

SERVES 4–6

2 tbsp olive oil

1 leek, sliced

1 onion, chopped

1 celery stalk, sliced

1 carrot, sliced

2 garlic cloves, crushed

1 tbsp coriander seeds

4 oz of canned tomatoes (½ cup)

5 oz of canned chickpeas (garbanzo
   beans), drained (½ cup)

4 cups vegetable stock

1 potato, cubed

2 bay leaves

pinch of saffron strands

2 lemons, halved, cut sides charred
   for 2–5 minutes in a hot
   nonstick skillet

Moroccan sauce

2 garlic cloves, finely sliced

½ red chile, finely chopped

1 tsp paprika

1 tsp ground cumin

1 tsp lemon juice

2 tsp white wine vinegar

¼ cup finely chopped fresh
   flat-leaf parsley

¼ cup finely chopped fresh
   cilantro leaves

Method

1 Heat the oil in a large saucepan and sauté the leek, onion, celery, carrot, and garlic, stirring continuously, for 5 minutes, or until softened but not colored. Add the coriander seeds and cook for an additional 2 minutes.

2 Add the tomatoes, chickpeas, stock, potato, bay leaves, and saffron. Stir well and bring to a boil. Reduce the heat, cover, and simmer for 20 minutes, or until the vegetables are tender.

3 To make the Moroccan sauce, pound the garlic and chile with the spices, lemon juice, and vinegar to a smooth paste in a mortar with a pestle. Transfer to a saucepan, add the herbs, and gently warm for 5 minutes to infuse the flavors. Do not boil.

4 Remove and discard the bay leaves, then blend the soup using a food processor or blender. Pass through a medium strainer into warm soup bowls. Top with the Moroccan sauce and serve with the charred lemons for squeezing over.

FREE-RANGE EGGS

03

Each egg is a microcosm of potential fertility. They contain the best sources of protein available when it comes to supporting both egg and sperm health.

Eggs encapsulate the possibility of new life, and so contain all the valuable nutrients needed to support it. Their balanced and rich fat content enables the production of the hormones estrogen and progesterone, needed for conception, and their record-breaking B-vitamin status helps a woman to use those hormones in the best way possible. High levels of selenium and sulfur also help to remove toxic metals, such as lead and mercury, which can interfere with fertility, while the vitamin A in eggs protects both egg and sperm from damage that can affect fertilization. Eggs contain both folate (folic acid) and choline, which have been shown to work together to prevent spina bifida and other neural tube defects in the fetus.

- Contain the right kind of fats, which act as building blocks in the body's production of fertility hormones.
- Sulfur and selenium remove toxic substances that can interfere with conception.
- Vitamin A and protein help keep eggs and sperm in optimum condition.
- Choline and folate content help prevent spina bifida.

Practical tips:
Buy organic free-range eggs where possible to avoid ingesting unwanted hormones that may interfere with conception and increase the risk of bacterial infection. Purchase from a reliable source. Having eggs for breakfast helps promote sustained energy levels.

DID YOU KNOW?

The high cholesterol level in eggs has not been shown to increase the risk of heart disease. This cholesterol is, in fact, necessary to make the fertility hormones estrogen and progesterone.

MAJOR NUTRIENTS PER MEDIUM-SIZE EGG

Calories	63
Total fat	4.37 g
Monounsaturated fat	1.68 g
Omega-6 fatty acids	505 mg
Omega-9 fatty acids	1,582 mg
Protein	5.53 g
Carbohydrate	0.34 g
Vitamin A	214 IU
Vitamin D	22 IU
Vitamin B2	0.21 mg
Vitamin B5	0.63 mg
Vitamin B12	0.57 mcg
Choline	110.5 mg
Iron	0.81 mg
Selenium	13.9 mcg
Zinc	0.49 mg
Lutein/Zeaxanthin	146 mcg

Tomato frittata

SERVES 4 (G) (A) (V) (Q)

6 extra-large eggs

2 tbsp chopped fresh basil

2 tbsp olive oil

1 small onion, sliced

2 large ripe tomatoes, halved,
seeded, and thinly sliced

pepper

arugula leaves, tossed in balsamic
vinegar and extra virgin olive oil,
to serve

Method

1 Beat the eggs in a bowl, then stir in the basil and season with pepper to taste; set aside.

2 Heat 1 tablespoon of the oil in a 10-inch nonstick skillet over medium heat. Add the onion and fry for 5–7 minutes, until softened but not browned.

3 Add the tomatoes to the skillet and fry for about 30 seconds, or until they start to soften. Carefully turn the onion and tomatoes into the bowl containing the eggs.

4 Wipe the skillet with paper towels and reheat over medium–high heat. Add the remaining oil and heat, swirling it around to coat the sides. Pour in the eggs and tomatoes and let cook for 5–6 minutes, shaking the skillet occasionally and working the set frittata into the center so the uncooked egg runs underneath.

5 Gently slide the frittata out of the skillet onto a large, flat plate. Place the skillet upside-down over the frittata, then, using an oven mitt, invert the skillet and plate, so that the uncooked side is on the bottom. Continue to cook for an additional 3–4 minutes, until the frittata is fully cooked and set throughout.

6 Slide the frittata onto a plate and serve warm, or let cool and serve at room temperature. Cut into wedges and serve with the dressed arugula leaves.

04 BROCCOLI

One of the true superfoods, broccoli has fantastic detoxifying qualities that help prepare a woman's reproductive system for conception and a healthy pregnancy.

All of the cruciferous (cabbage family) vegetables—broccoli, Brussels sprouts, cabbage, cauliflower, bok choy, and kale—contain sulfur-base chemicals called glucosinolates, which help rid the body of harmful substances, such as pollutants and toxic metals. These can build up in the reproductive system of both men and women and may reduce your chances of fertility. Glucosinolates also promote balance between the female sex hormones estrogen and progesterone, which support a healthy menstrual cycle and a woman's chances of conception. Add in vitamin C, vitamin E, and the carotenoids lutein and beta-carotene for antioxidant protection against damage to egg and sperm, and broccoli provides you with the complete cleansing package. The high levels of folate (folic acid) also help prevent birth defects and premature birth.

DID YOU KNOW?

The strong green color of broccoli is proof of the concentrated amounts of chlorophyll used by the plant to trap energy from the sun. Chlorophyll has long been used by traditional healers to "nourish the blood," thereby promoting fertility.

MAJOR NUTRIENTS PER 100 G/ABOUT 1½ CUPS BROCCOLI

Calories	34
Total fat	0.37 g
Protein	2.82 g
Carbohydrate	6.64 g
Fiber	2.6 g
Vitamin C	89.2 mg
Vitamin A	623 IU
Vitamin E	0.78 mg
Folate	90 mcg
Beta-carotene	361 mcg
Lutein/Zeaxanthin	1,121 mcg

- Contains glucosinolates and fiber, which remove harmful, antifertility substances from the body.
- Sulfur compounds also balance hormones for conception.
- Contains high levels of protective antioxidants, which prevent damage to both egg and sperm.
- Provides folate, needed in preparation for a healthy, full-term pregnancy.

Practical tips:

To preserve both the taste and nutrients of broccoli, steam or lightly stir-fry, and be careful not to overcook. Try different varieties and enjoy broccoli simply, with olive oil and lemon juice.

Broccoli and snow pea stir-fry

SERVES 4 (G) (A) (V) (Q)

2 tbsp vegetable or peanut oil

1 garlic clove, finely chopped

3 cups small broccoli florets

2 cups trimmed snow peas

2½ cups Chinese cabbage, cut into
½-inch slices

5–6 scallions, finely chopped

2 tbsp light soy sauce

1 tsp sesame oil

1 tsp sesame seeds, lightly toasted

Method

1 In a preheated wok, heat the oil, then add the garlic and stir-fry
for 30 seconds. Add all the vegetables and stir-fry over high
heat for 3 minutes.

2 Pour in the soy sauce and sesame oil and cook for an additional
minute. Sprinkle with the sesame seeds and serve hot.

05 CAULIFLOWER

Like its other cruciferous cousins, cauliflower contains sulfur compounds that support detoxification and help balance female hormones ready for conception.

As one of the cruciferous (cabbage family) vegetables, along with broccoli, cabbage, kale, bok choy, and Brussels sprouts, cauliflower contains the chemical di-indolylmethane (DIM), which may help your body use estrogen more efficiently and support the chances of fertility. Cauliflower is one of the important foods to include in a fertility diet to help the liver process and eliminate toxins that may interfere with reproduction. The antioxidant vitamin C increases the effect of other antioxidants consumed to support detoxification. Vitamin C also supports the immune system to protect against infectious bacteria that may affect fertility. Cauliflower contains the two B vitamins folate (folic acid) and choline, which help protect against the likelihood of spina bifida or neural tube defect in the embryo.

- DIM helps utilize estrogen to the best advantage for pregnancy to occur.
- Sulfur compounds and vitamin C support detoxification and immunity to optimize fertility.
- Folate and choline work together to help lessen the risk of neural tube defect.

DID YOU KNOW?

Cauliflower works very well in curries, and particularly with the anti-inflammatory and detoxifying spice turmeric for a great fertility combination to prepare your body for conception.

MAJOR NUTRIENTS PER 100 G/ABOUT ¾ CUP CAULIFLOWER

Calories	25
Total fat	0.28 g
Protein	1.92 g
Carbohydrate	4.97 g
Fiber	2.0 g
Vitamin C	48.2 mg
Vitamin K	28.5 mcg
Folate	57 mcg
Choline	44.3 mg
Potassium	299 mg

Practical tips:

Cauliflower can suffer from overcooking and become mushy; to avoid this, stir-fry instead of boiling or steaming. Boiling cauliflower for longer than five minutes has shown a significant reduction in nutrients; these are retained well when steaming or stir-frying.

Cauliflower soup

SERVES 6   (G) (A) (V)

1 tbsp olive oil
2 tbsp butter
1 large onion, coarsely chopped
2 leeks, sliced
1 large cauliflower
3½ cups vegetable stock
salt and pepper
finely grated cheddar cheese and
   extra virgin olive oil, to serve

Method

1 Heat the olive oil and butter in a large saucepan and fry the onion and leeks for 10 minutes, stirring frequently, being careful not to let the vegetables color.

2 Cut the cauliflower into florets and cut the stalk into small pieces. Add to the pan and sauté with the other vegetables for 2–3 minutes.

3 Add the stock and bring to a boil, cover, and simmer over medium heat for 20 minutes.

4 Pour the soup into a food processor or blender, process until smooth, and return to the rinsed-out saucepan. Heat the soup through, season to taste with salt and pepper, and serve in warm soup bowls topped with a spoonful of grated cheese and a drizzle of extra virgin olive oil.

06 BUCKWHEAT

Buckwheat provides a rich helping of the B vitamins and magnesium vital for energy, sex drive, and fertility. Any food that can give these a boost is one to remember!

B vitamins and magnesium are needed to produce energy in our cells, making them essential to the creation of new life. In addition, they help us cope with stress—anxiety has been shown to be a major barrier to conception. Buckwheat is also a very good source of slow-release energy, so its inclusion in the diet helps prevent the blood sugar highs and lows that can rob would-be parents of the energy needed for procreation. It is an excellent source of rutin, a circulation-boosting antioxidant that carries blood supply, energy, and nutrients to the reproductive areas. These areas are further protected by the cleansing capacity of buckwheat, along with its zinc and selenium content, which can help prevent damage caused by pollution, harmful chemicals, and some medications. Zinc and selenium are very often found to be low in women and men who are infertile.

- B vitamins and magnesium help keep up energy levels and combat stress, which can interfere with fertility.
- Contains rutin, which supports circulation and, therefore, blood and oxygen flow to reproductive areas.
- Antioxidants zinc and selenium support fertility levels and prevent damage by environmental toxins.

Practical tips:
Use buckwheat flour to make pancakes. Buckwheat is often found in wheat-free products, but its lack of gluten means it doesn't produce the "fluffiness" considered desirable in many breads.

DID YOU KNOW?

Buckwheat is actually a fruit seed and much easier to digest than a grain. As such, it is less likely to cause any intolerance or inflammation that may interfere with your chances of fertility.

MAJOR NUTRIENTS PER 100 G/ABOUT ½ CUP BUCKWHEAT GRAINS

Calories	343
Total fat	3.4 g
Omega-6 fatty acids	1,052 mg
Protein	13.25 g
Carbohydrate	71.5 g
Fiber	10 g
Vitamin B2	0.43 mg
Vitamin B3	7.02 mg
Vitamin B5	1.23 mg
Vitamin B6	0.21 g
Magnesium	231 g
Potassium	460 mg
Manganese	1.33 mg
Selenium	8.3 g
Zinc	2.4 mg

Buckwheat crepes

MAKES 10 (A)(V)(Q)

3 cups buckwheat flour
pinch of sea salt (optional)
1¾ cups milk
about 1 cup water
about 5 tbsp butter, melted
2 tsp olive oil
cherry tomatoes, to garnish

Filling

1 cup ricotta cheese
4 large charbroiled red bell
*   peppers in olive oil, drained*
*   and thinly sliced*
3 tbsp chopped fresh basil
pepper

Method

1 Sift the flour and salt into a large mixing bowl, then make a well in the center. Add half of the milk and gradually stir into the flour to make a thick, smooth batter. Gradually beat in the remaining milk. Cover the bowl with plastic wrap and set aside to rest for 45 minutes.

2 Uncover the batter and beat in ⅔ cup of water, then slowly beat in more water until the batter is the consistency of light cream. Add half of the butter and beat until incorporated.

3 Heat a 9-inch nonstick skillet over medium–high heat until hot. Add the oil and swirl the skillet until it coats the surface. Reduce the heat to medium. Rub the surface of the skillet with a little of the remaining butter. Drop a small ladleful of batter in the center of the skillet and immediately lift and tilt the pan so the batter covers the bottom as thinly as possible. Cook the crepe until it is golden brown with holes starting to appear on the surface, then flip it over, using a spatula. Cook until the other side is set, then transfer to a plate and keep warm. Repeat until all the batter is used.

4 Arrange the crepes on the work surface, then divide the ricotta, red bell peppers, and basil among them. Season with pepper and turn the sides of each crepe into the center, then fold in at the ends to make a square package.

5 Reheat the skillet. Rub with the remaining butter, add the crepes, folded side down, and cook for 90 seconds, then flip over and cook for an additional 30 seconds, or until the crepes are hot and the filling warmed through. Serve hot, garnished with the cherry tomatoes.

07

GUAVA

The antioxidants in guava protect every part of the body from free-radical damage. This damage can penetrate our DNA and affect our ability to reproduce.

Free radicals come from sunlight, pollution, fried food, and even the essential process of creating energy. Free-radical damage occurs in every part of our body all the time, and we need a constant and varied supply of antioxidants to stop it from causing harm and to protect the egg and sperm from damage. The fiber in guava also carries toxins out of the body. Guava is especially supportive of sperm health, because vitamin C increases the number of sperm produced, beta-carotene boosts their concentration, vitamin E aids their ability to travel, and zinc improves their quality. All these antioxidants protect the egg, too, and make it ripe for fertilization. The zinc in guava aids normal fetal development, and the antioxidant proanthocyanidin, which helps to make the guava flesh red, encourages blood to flow to the penis.

- High-antioxidant levels and fiber protect both egg and sperm from the free-radical damage that naturally occurs every day.
- Contains a range of nutrients, including vitamins C and E, that help create healthy sperm, able to travel to and fertilize the egg.
- Proanthocyanidin supports blood flow to the male reproductive area, enabling sexual function.

Practical tips:
When selecting guavas, avoid any that are spotty, mushy, or very green and choose those that are yellowish in color and that yield slightly when pressed. Eat on its own as a snack, or use as any other fruit; try it juiced, in salads, or with cereal.

DID YOU KNOW?

The red flesh of the guava is the clue to the rich fat-soluble antioxidants it contains. Lycopene, beta-carotene, and vitamin E all help to support the environment in which sperm are stored and carried.

MAJOR NUTRIENTS PER MEDIUM-SIZE GUAVA

Calories	37
Total fat	0.52 g
Protein	1.4 g
Carbohydrate	7.88 g
Fiber	3 g
Vitamin C	125.6 mg
Vitamin E	0.4 mg
Zinc	0.13 mg
Beta-carotene	206 mcg
Lycopene	2,862 mcg

Guava smoothie

SERVES 2   (G) (A) (V) (Q)

14 oz of canned guavas, drained
(2½ cups)
1 cup ice-cold milk

Method

1 Place the guavas in a food processor or blender and pour in the milk.
2 Process until well blended.
3 Strain into glasses to remove the hard seeds. Serve.

08 LAMB

Lamb is a dense, good-quality protein meat with a useful vitamin-B profile. Consumed in moderation, it can help the body make the structures and cells needed for fertility.

MAJOR NUTRIENTS PER 100 G/3½ oz LAMB

Calories	229
Total fat	16.97 g
Saturated fat	8.18 g
Monounsaturated fat	6.91 g
Protein	17.84 g
Carbohydrate	0 g
Fiber	0 g
Vitamin B2	0.26 mg
Vitamin B3	4.93 mg
Vitamin B5	0.56 mg
Vitamin B6	0.34 mg
Vitamin B12	2.47 mcg
Iron	1.43 mg
Zinc	3.67 mg
Selenium	7.5 mcg

Lamb provides all nine of the amino acids, the protein building blocks necessary for healthy sperm, womb lining, and cell replication, as well as the B vitamins needed to make these new proteins. It also contains good levels of the antioxidant trace minerals selenium and zinc, which protect the egg, sperm, and uterus from damage and help the liver remove the toxins that can interfere with reproductive processes. Zinc deficiency has been linked to infertility and miscarriage, because zinc is needed for all body tissues and organisms to grow. Lamb also provides another antioxidant, coenzyme-Q10, that may help conception by improving blood supply and energy in cells within the reproductive organs.

- A good-quality protein that also contains the B vitamins, promoting a healthy uterus, sperm, and efficient cell division, all of which encourages chances of conception.
- Contains the antioxidants zinc and selenium, which protect the reproductive organs from damage.
- Coenzyme-Q10 content supports a healthy blood supply and energy within the reproductive system.

Practical tips:
Lamb contains high levels of saturated fat, so do not eat more than once a week. Chops are the healthiest cuts. Choose free-range, organic lamb, if possible, to ensure the best-quality fats and minimum levels of damaging hormones and chemicals.

Stir-fried lamb with orange

SERVES 4 Ⓖ Ⓐ Ⓠ

1 tbsp vegetable or peanut oil
1 lb ground lamb
2 garlic cloves, crushed
1 tsp cumin seeds
1 tsp ground coriander
1 red onion, finely sliced
grated rind and juice of 1 orange
2 tbsp soy sauce
1 orange, peeled and segmented
pepper
snipped fresh chives, to garnish

Method

1 Heat a wok or large, nonstick skillet. Add the oil and lamb and stir-fry for 5 minutes, or until evenly browned. Drain away any excess fat from the wok.

2 Add the garlic, cumin seeds, coriander, and red onion to the wok and stir-fry for an additional 5 minutes.

3 Stir in the orange rind and juice and the soy sauce, mixing until thoroughly combined. Cover, reduce the heat, and simmer, stirring occasionally, for 15 minutes.

4 Remove the lid, increase the heat, and add the orange segments. Stir to mix.

5 Season with pepper and heat through for an additional 2–3 minutes. Serve immediately, garnished with chives.

09

MILK

Milk provides a complete protein source, supplying the building blocks needed for conception, to make new sperm, and for a healthy womb lining.

This versatile food is particularly good for vegetarians, who do not have many other sources of complete protein in their diet. Milk also supplies the body with the macrominerals calcium, potassium, and phosphorus, which are needed in large amounts for a growing baby's skeleton. A lack of these minerals in the mother can increase a baby's risk of growth and development problems and impaired muscular function, so it is important to keep up maternal intake. Increasing calcium intake before pregnancy has been shown to reduce risk of hypertension (high blood pressure), and the related complication preeclampsia, later in pregnancy.

- A complete protein that is suitable for vegetarians, which enables the body to create sperm and the new cells needed for reproduction.
- Helps the mother-to-be stock up on calcium, potassium, and phosphorus in anticipation of the baby's bone growth and development.
- Calcium helps reduce the risk of high blood pressure developing later in pregnancy.

Practical tips:
You won't get the goodness of milk by using it in tea or coffee, because the potentially damaging effects of caffeine outweigh its benefits. Enjoy it on cereal or in a smoothie, and don't overdo milk consumption if you tend to get nasal or digestive problems.

DID YOU KNOW?

Choosing organic milk will reduce the amount of hormones and antibiotics you take into your body. These are regularly added to the feed of cows on nonorganic farms, and can interfere with the ability to conceive.

MAJOR NUTRIENTS PER 100 ML/ABOUT 7 TBSP LOWFAT MILK

Calories	50
Total fat	3.33 g
Protein	3.33 g
Carbohydrate	6.66 g
Vitamin D	43.66 IU
Betaine	1 mg
Choline	16.66 mg
Calcium	119 mg
Potassium	152.66 mg

Spiced banana milkshake

SERVES 2

1½ cups milk

2 bananas

⅔ cup plain yogurt with
  live cultures

½ tsp pumpkin pie spice, plus extra
  to decorate

6 ice cubes (optional)

Method

1 Place the milk, bananas, yogurt, and pumpkin pie spice in a food
  processor or blender and process gently until smooth.

2 Pour the mixture into two glasses and serve with ice, if using.
  Add a pinch of pumpkin pie spice to decorate.

10

SUN-DRIED TOMATOES

The antioxidants in sun-dried tomatoes are mainly fat soluble, which means they protect fatty areas of the body, including the reproductive organs, eggs, and sperm.

DID YOU KNOW?

Lycopene levels in processed tomatoes can be up to ten times higher than in the raw fruit, which makes sun-dried tomatoes an excellent choice for would-be fathers. These naturally dried versions are also a much healthier way of receiving the benefits of tomatoes compared to high sugar, processed tomato-base foods, such as ketchup.

MAJOR NUTRIENTS PER 100 G /ABOUT 1¾ CUPS SUN-DRIED TOMATOES, WITHOUT OIL

Calories	258
Total fat	2.97 g
Protein	14.11 g
Carbohydrate	55.76 g
Fiber	12.3 g
Vitamin C	39.2 mg
Vitamin A	874 IU
Magnesium	194 mg
Potassium	3,427 mg
Sodium	2,095 mg
Lycopene	45,902 mcg
Beta-carotene	524 mcg
Lutein/Zeaxanthin	1,419 mcg

Lycopene and other fat-soluble antioxidant carotenoids, such as beta-carotene, lutein, and zeaxanthin, are found in large concentrations in healthy testes. Lycopene has been shown to support male fertility, particularly because it plays a part in correcting low sperm count and even abnormal sperm. Tomatoes, or other deep, rich colored vegetables, need to be eaten daily in order to keep these antioxidant levels up and capable of protecting healthy sperm from damage. The essential minerals sodium and potassium are also provided in good amounts by this fruit, keeping our bodies alkalized and hydrated, and ensuring the efficient removal of toxins that may prevent conception.

• Lycopene is particularly important for ensuring good levels of healthy, active sperm.
• Contain fat-soluble carotenoids that ensure the male testes are the best possible breeding ground for sperm.
• The right balance of sodium and potassium ensures the removal of toxins that can affect fertility.

Practical tips:
The table of major nutrients on this page refers only to the dried tomatoes themselves, but you can receive extra benefits by eating sun-dried tomatoes that are sold in a good-quality extra virgin olive oil. The oil provides oleic acid, which moves the essential fatty acids and carotenoids that help to keep us fertile into our cells.

Asparagus and sun-dried tomato risotto

SERVES 4 (A)

4 cups vegetable stock

1 tbsp olive oil

3 tbsp butter

1 small onion, finely chopped

6 sun-dried tomatoes, thinly sliced

1½ cups risotto rice

⅔ cup alcohol-free dry
white wine

8 oz fresh asparagus spears,
cooked

pepper

freshly grated Parmesan cheese
and finely grated lemon rind,
to serve

Method

1 Bring the stock to a boil in a saucepan, then reduce the heat and simmer over low heat while you cook the risotto.

2 Heat the oil with 1 tablespoon of the butter in a deep saucepan over medium heat until the butter has melted. Stir in the onion and sun-dried tomatoes, and cook, stirring occasionally, for 5 minutes, until the onion is soft and starting to turn golden. Do not brown.

3 Reduce the heat, add the rice, and mix to coat the grains in oil and butter. Cook, stirring continuously, for 2–3 minutes, or until the rice is translucent. Add the wine and cook, stirring continuously, until reduced.

4 Gradually add the hot stock, a ladleful at a time. Stir continuously and add more liquid as the rice absorbs each addition. Increase the heat to medium so that the liquid simmers. Cook for 20 minutes, or until all the liquid is absorbed and the rice is creamy. Season with pepper to taste.

5 While the risotto is cooking, set aside 4 asparagus spears (to garnish) and cut the remaining spears into 1-inch long pieces. Carefully fold the sliced asparagus into the risotto for the last 5 minutes of cooking time.

6 Remove the risotto from the heat and add the remaining butter. Mix well. Spoon the risotto into warm serving dishes and garnish with the reserved asparagus. Sprinkle some Parmesan and lemon rind on top, then serve.

11 QUINOA

Quinoa provides all of the essential amino acids needed to make proteins, which are crucial for reproduction. It also has a rich mineral and B-vitamin content.

MAJOR NUTRIENTS PER 100 G/ABOUT ½ CUP UNCOOKED QUINOA

Calories	368
Total fat	6.07 g
Omega-6 fatty acids	2,977 mg
Protein	14.12 g
Carbohydrate	64.16 g
Fiber	7 g
Vitamin B1	0.36 mg
Vitamin B2	0.32 mg
Vitamin B3	1.52 mg
Vitamin B5	0.77 mg
Vitamin B6	0.49 mg
Folate	184 mcg
Magnesium	197 mg
Iron	4.57 mg
Manganese	2.03 mg
Selenium	8.5 mcg
Zinc	3.1 mg

Low protein levels can interfere with the frequency of the menstrual cycle and also the quality of sperm, both of which can lead to lower chances of conception. This complete protein from the plant kingdom is more alkalizing than animal sources of protein, so it helps maintain the slightly alkaline environment needed for a healthy egg and womb. This environment is also vital in the male reproductive system, in order for sperm to flourish and then be able to travel and fertilize the egg inside the woman. Omega-6 fatty acids keep all the cells concerned supple and intact and, along with the B vitamins, maintain the balance of female and male sex hormones necessary for conception. The folate (folic acid) and zinc in quinoa also work together to allow reproduction to occur and prepare the body for a healthy full-term pregnancy.

• Complete protein that supports healthy periods and sperm.
• Contains omega-6 fatty acids and the B vitamins to support sex hormone levels in both women and men.
• Folate and zinc combine to enable the new cell production needed for conception.

Practical tips:

Quinoa can be used like a grain but is actually a seed, which makes it very easy on the digestion. It soaks up other flavors well and can be used as a salad base or a sweet hot cereal with fruit. For a protein boost, you can also try adding it to smoothies.

Quinoa and walnut salad

SERVES 2 (G)(V)(Q)

½ cup quinoa

1 cup water

1 zucchini, coarsely grated

2 large scallions, thinly sliced
    diagonally

handful fresh mint leaves, chopped

handful fresh flat-leaf parsley
    leaves, chopped

8 walnut halves, chopped

Dressing

3 tbsp extra virgin olive oil

1 tbsp lemon juice

1 tsp Dijon mustard

1 garlic clove, crushed

pepper

Method

1 Put the quinoa in a saucepan and pour over the water. Bring to a boil, reduce the heat to its lowest setting, cover with a lid, and simmer for about 15 minutes, until the water has been absorbed and the grains are tender. Set aside, covered, for 5 minutes.

2 Transfer the quinoa to a bowl and add the zucchini, scallions, mint, and parsley.

3 Mix together the ingredients for the dressing, then pour over the salad. Turn gently until combined.

4 Sprinkle with the walnuts just before serving at room temperature.

12 RADISH

Radish helps balance hormones and detoxify the body. The chemical raphanin supports thyroid health, helping would-be parents maintain energy levels.

All of the cruciferous (cabbage family) vegetables provide sulfur compounds, such as glucosinolates, that balance estrogen and progesterone in women, enabling healthy ovulation and fertilization, and later the ability to support the growing fetus in the womb. Radish comes with the added bonus of supporting the thyroid gland, which plays a part in regulating these hormones over the course of the menstrual cycle. Glucosinolates also help remove xenoestrogens from the body; found in plastics and tap water, these can mimic and disrupt our body's natural hormones. The folate (folic acid) and calcium in radish further prepare the body to support a healthy fetus and take it to full term in a successful pregnancy.

- Sulfur-containing glucosinolates optimize the balance of hormones prior to pregnancy, and help remove xenoestrogens, which can interfere with this balance.
- Contains raphanin, which supports thyroid health, providing energy for procreation and reproduction, and helping to regulate sex hormones.
- Guards against folate and calcium deficiencies that can have a detrimental effect on fertility and jeopardize pregnancy.

Practical tips:
Add radishes to salads—their sharp, crisp taste will help the digestive juices flow. They can also be added to juices. Try more exotic varieties, if available, such as daikon.

DID YOU KNOW?

If you are prone to constipation, limit your chances of developing hemorrhoids in pregnancy by eating radishes now. Vitamin C, fiber, and liver support will help prevent toxic buildup in the colon and heal tissues.

MAJOR NUTRIENTS PER 2 RADISHES

Calories	2
Total fat	0 g
Protein	0.06 g
Carbohydrate	0.30 g
Fiber	0.2 g
Vitamin C	1.4 mg
Folate	2 mcg
Potassium	20 mg
Calcium	2 mg

Chicken and radish salad

SERUES 2

2 skinless, boneless chicken
breasts, about 6 oz each
2 tbsp olive oil
2 tsp dried thyme
2 tsp ground coriander
½ cup frozen soybeans (edamame)
1 small Boston lettuce, leaves
separated
¾ cup diagonally sliced snow peas
1 large scallion, thinly sliced
diagonally
5 radishes, sliced into rounds
pepper

Dressing

handful fresh mint leaves
6 tbsp plain yogurt with live cultures
juice of ½ lime
½ tsp cumin seeds
pepper

Method

1 Using a meat mallet or the end of a rolling pin, flatten the chicken
until about ½ inch thick. Pour the oil into a large, shallow bowl
and stir in the thyme and coriander. Season with pepper, add the
chicken, and turn until coated.

2 Heat a ridged grill pan over medium–high heat. Grill the chicken
for 6 minutes, turning once, until cooked through and golden.

3 Cook the soybeans in a little boiling water for 3–4 minutes, or until
tender. Drain and refresh under cold running water.

4 Using a food processor or blender, mix together the first three
ingredients for the dressing. Transfer to a bowl, season with pepper,
and scatter over the cumin seeds.

5 Divide the lettuce between two large, shallow bowls, then top with
the snow peas, scallion, radishes, and soybeans. Slice the chicken
lengthwise and arrange on top of the salad. Spoon the dressing
over before serving.

13 MACKEREL

Mackerel provides essential omega-3 fatty acids, which ensure the correct fat balance in the cells of sperm, egg, and womb. These also help to balance female sex hormones.

It is difficult to underestimate the importance of omega-3 fatty acids in our diets in terms of supporting fertility and also the developing brain of the fetus. In mackerel, and other oily fish, these fatty acids take the form of DHA (docosahexaenoic acid) and EPA (eicosapentaenoic acid) and help to balance out any excess of omega-6 fatty acids, which our bodies take in the modern diet from grains and nuts. DHA and EPA help us cope with stress, too, through the production of the "happy" brain chemicals serotonin and dopamine, which support libido. Stress reduction is a key component in addressing fertility issues. The high protein and vitamin-B levels in mackerel add to the stress-reducing effect by helping to balance blood sugar and create the energy needed for reproduction.

- Omega-3 fatty acids DHA and EPA support reproductive systems and balance out the hormones needed to make these work.
- Omega-3 fatty acids also support healthy sexual function.
- Omega-3 fatty acids, alongside protein and the B vitamins, help reduce stress reactions and boost energy levels ready for fertility.

DID YOU KNOW?

Some scientists believe that it was our ancestors' consumption of oily fish that contributed to the human brain developing the conscious and cognitive thought processes that we take for granted today.

MAJOR NUTRIENTS PER 100 G/3½ OZ FRESH MACKEREL

Calories	105
Total fat	2 g
Omega-3 fatty acids—EPA	0.136 g
Omega-3 fatty acids—DHA	0.18 g
Protein	20.28 g
Vitamin B3	8.6 mg
Vitamin A	727 IU

Practical tips:
Mackerel is one of the safer oily fish to eat because it contains very low levels of mercury, which is shown to directly affect fertility in both men and women. However, do not eat more than 12 oz of fish a week during pregnancy, and avoid king mackerel entirely.

Spiced mackerel with tomato salad

SERVES 4 Ⓖ Ⓐ Ⓠ

4 garlic cloves, crushed

finely grated zest and juice
   of 1 lemon

heaping 1 tsp ground cumin

heaping 1 tsp smoked paprika

2–3 tbsp olive oil

4 large mackerel fillets, about
   6 oz each, or 8 small mackerel
   fillets, about 3 oz each

Tomato salad

3 medium juicy ripe tomatoes,
   sliced

1 small red onion, thinly sliced

heaping 1 tbsp chopped fresh
   herbs, such as thyme, mint,
   or parsley

2 tbsp olive oil

1 tbsp white wine vinegar

pepper

Method

1 Mix together the garlic, lemon zest and juice, cumin, paprika, and oil in a small bowl. Put the mackerel fillets in a shallow, nonmetallic dish and thoroughly rub both sides with the spice mixture. Cover and let marinate in a cool place for 30 minutes, if possible.

2 Preheat the broiler to high. Lay the mackerel fillets in the broiler pan and cook under the preheated broiler for 3 minutes on one side, then turn over, drizzle with any remaining marinade, and cook for another 2–3 minutes, or until the mackerel is cooked through.

3 Meanwhile, prepare the tomato salad. Arrange the tomatoes and onion on a serving platter. Put the herbs, oil, and vinegar in a screw-top jar and shake well to combine. Season with pepper to taste.

4 Drizzle the dressing over the tomato salad and serve with the hot mackerel fillets.

14

CILANTRO LEAVES

The leaves from the coriander plant, cilantro has been shown to remove toxic metals from our bodies. The absence of these metals improves chances of conception.

Heavy metal toxicity, even at low levels, can affect men and women profoundly. Mercury from fillings, tuna, and vaccinations has been most frequently associated with female infertility. Male infertility has been predominantly linked to lead, found in pollution, cigarette smoke, and old pipes. Toxic metals can hide in the reproductive organs without affecting our day-to-day bodily systems. The antioxidant nutrients vitamins A and C and carotenoids beta-carotene, lutein, and zeaxanthin in cilantro support the plant's ability to remove toxic metals by protecting the cells and tissues they can harm. Cilantro has also been shown to protect calcium levels in the body by reducing the lead buildup in bone.

- Effectively and safely removes toxic metals, such as mercury and lead, that are linked to female and male infertility.
- High antioxidant levels protect the body tissues as toxic metals leave the body.
- Helps restore calcium levels in bone by removing lead.
- The fragrant volatile oils are antimicrobials, which help destroy immune-stressing invaders.

Practical tips:
Add fresh cilantro to salads, and use to garnish soups, stews, and curries just before serving to preserve the nutrients. Add a handful to a juice or smoothie or create a simple pesto by adding a few chopped teaspoons to Brazil nuts, olive oil, and garlic.

DID YOU KNOW?

The fragrant aroma from cilantro leaves heralds the potency of their pungent oils. As strong antimicrobial agents, these oils ward off infections that can interfere with conception.

MAJOR NUTRIENTS PER 15 G/ABOUT 1 CUP CILANTRO

Calories	3.45
Total fat	0.08 g
Protein	0.32 g
Carbohydrate	0.55 g
Fiber	0.42 g
Vitamin C	4.05 mg
Vitamin A	1,012.2 IU
Vitamin K	46.5 mcg
Beta-carotene	589.5 mcg
Lutein/Zeaxanthin	129.75 mcg

Turkey skewers with cilantro pesto

SERVES 4   (A) (N)

1 lb skinless, boneless turkey, cut
    into 2-inch cubes
2 zucchini, thickly sliced
1 red and 1 yellow bell pepper,
    seeded and cut into 2-inch
    squares
8 cherry tomatoes
8 pearl onions, peeled
    but left whole

Marinade

4 tbsp olive oil
2 tsp Dijon mustard
1 tsp green peppercorns, crushed
2 tbsp chopped fresh cilantro

Cilantro pesto

3½ cups fresh cilantro
15 fresh parsley sprigs
1 garlic clove
½ cup pine nuts
¼ cup freshly grated Parmesan
    cheese
6 tbsp extra virgin olive oil
juice of 1 lemon

Method

1 Place the turkey in a large bowl. To make the marinade, mix the
olive oil, mustard, peppercorns, and cilantro together in a pitcher.
Pour the mixture over the turkey and turn until the turkey is
thoroughly coated. Cover with plastic wrap and let marinate in the
refrigerator for 2 hours.

2 Preheat the broiler to medium–high. To make the cilantro pesto, put
the cilantro and parsley into a food processor and process until finely
chopped. Add the garlic and pine nuts and pulse until chopped. Add
the Parmesan, oil, and lemon juice and process briefly to mix. Transfer
to a bowl, cover, and let chill in the refrigerator until required.

3 Thread the turkey (reserving the marinade), zucchini, bell peppers,
cherry tomatoes, and onions alternately onto presoaked wooden
skewers. Broil under medium–high heat, turning and brushing
frequently with the marinade, for 10–12 minutes. Serve immediately
with the cilantro pesto.

15

CINNAMON

Cinnamon is a powerful spice and a traditional aphrodisiac. It also helps reduce cravings for sweet foods that rob us of the nutrients we need for reproduction.

The active compound in cinnamon, methylhydroxychalcone polymer (MHCP), acts in the same way as the hormone insulin, taking sugars from dietary sources from the bloodstream into our cells to be used as energy. Eating too many refined sugars in the form of cakes, biscuits and sweets causes sudden surges of sugar into the bloodstream and sets up a cycle of sugar highs and lows, whereby the body regularly craves sugar and often caffeine in order to pull itself out of an energy slump. Just half a teaspoon of cinnamon per day has been shown to decrease excess blood sugar and put an end to these cravings. Cinnamon is also a strong antioxidant and works hard to protect the body from damage.

- Contains the substance MHCP, which evens out blood sugar levels and supports a sustained release of energy.
- Breaks the cycles of dependence on sugar, caffeine and other stimulants that undermine fertility.
- Its powerful antioxidant properties help prevent and even repair damage caused by excess dietary sugars.

Practical tips:
Powdered cinnamon spice is stronger than the stick form, but it does not stay fresh for as long – replace when the characteristic smell has faded. Cinnamon naturally sweetens food, so add to juices, porridge, yogurt or cereal. Do not take supplements or consume cinnamon in large amounts during pregnancy.

DID YOU KNOW?

In traditional Chinese medicine, cinnamon is used to treat infertility by increasing male yang energy, and by increasing blood flow to the reproductive organs in both sexes.

MAJOR NUTRIENTS PER 15 G/½ OZ GROUND CINNAMON (CASSIA)

Kcalories	37
Total fat	0.19 g
Protein	0.59 g
Carbohydrate	12.09 g
Fibre	7.97 g
Vitamin C	0.57 mg
Vitamin A	44.25 IU
Calcium	150.3 mg
Manganese	2.62 mg

Cinnamon, apple, and blackberry crunch

SERVES 2

2 apples, peeled, cored, and diced

½ cup water

½ cup rolled oats

1 tsp ground cinnamon, plus extra
   for sprinkling

3 tsp honey

1 cup blackberries

1 cup Greek yogurt with live cultures

2 tbsp slivered almonds

Method

1 Put the apples and the water in a saucepan and stew, covered, for 10–12 minutes, until tender. Mash with the back of a fork or potato masher to make a coarse applesauce.

2 Meanwhile, toast the oats in a large, dry, nonstick skillet for 5 minutes, tossing regularly, until light golden. Remove from the skillet and let cool.

3 When the apples are cooked, stir in the cinnamon, 2 teaspoons of the honey, and the blackberries.

4 To serve, put one-quarter of the oats in each of 2 large wine glasses or bowls. Top each with one-quarter of the yogurt, then half of the fruit mixture, followed by half of the remaining yogurt. Divide the rest of the oats, scatter over the tops, and drizzle with the honey. To finish, sprinkle with a little extra cinnamon and the almonds.

16

MISO

In Japanese culture, miso has a long association with female health and fertility. Most Japanese include it in the diet several times a week.

Miso is made by fermenting soybeans. In common with other traditional fermented food, such as yogurt, it can help support the immune and digestive systems, which keeps bacteria from causing harm and interfering with fertility. Miso also contains a plant form of estrogen that cleverly adjusts the levels in our body if they are too high or too low. This effect can be thrown out of balance, however, if too much is eaten. Miso also contains vitamin K, which is needed to transport calcium to our bones. A prospective mother needs to be sure she has optimum levels of calcium before pregnancy so that her stores don't get depleted by the growing baby's skeleton.

- A fermented food that supports good digestion and encourages our immune system to ward off harmful infections.
- A plant form of estrogen that can help correct sex hormone imbalances when eaten a few times a week.
- Contains vitamin K, which helps calcium to mineralize into bone in preparation for good mother and baby bone health.

Practical tips:
The most common form of miso (hatcho) is made from soybeans and this has the highest hormone-balancing effect. If you are intolerant to soybeans, try rice, barley, or wheat misos. The paste form is far superior to the powder. Make a simple miso soup by boiling dark leafy greens lightly in water and adding paste to taste. Miso is high in sodium, so use it in moderation.

DID YOU KNOW?

Although soybean products have been the subject of controversy, natural, fermented soybean foods, such as miso and tempeh, have been shown to support fertility.

MAJOR NUTRIENTS PER 15 ML/1 TBSP MISO

Calories	34
Total fat	1.03 g
Protein	2.01 g
Carbohydrate	4.55 g
Fiber	0.93 g
Vitamin B1	0.02 mg
Vitamin B2	0.04 mg
Vitamin B3	0.16 mg
Vitamin B5	0.06 mg
Vitamin B6	0.03 mg
Vitamin B12	0.01 mcg
Vitamin K	4.98 mcg
Iron	0.43 mg
Selenium	1.2 mcg
Zinc	0.44 mg

Miso fish soup

SERVES 4   (G) (A) (N) (Q)

3½ cups fish stock or vegetable
   stock
1-inch piece fresh ginger, peeled
   and grated
1 tbsp Thai fish sauce
1 red chile, seeded and finely sliced
1 carrot, thinly sliced
½ cup thin daikon thin strips,
   or ½ bunch radishes, trimmed
   and sliced
1 yellow bell pepper, seeded
   and cut into thin strips
3 oz shiitake mushrooms,
   sliced if large
1½ oz fine egg noodles
8 oz sole fillets, skinned and
   cut into strips
1 tbsp miso paste
4 scallions, trimmed and shredded

Method

1 Pour the stock into a large saucepan and add the ginger, fish sauce,
   and chile. Bring to a boil, then reduce the heat and simmer for
   5 minutes.

2 Add the carrot with the daikon, bell pepper, mushrooms, and
   noodles and simmer for an additional 3 minutes.

3 Add the fish strips with the miso paste and continue to cook for
   2 minutes, or until the fish is tender. Divide equally among 4 warm
   soup bowls, top with the scallions, and serve.

17 PEARS

Pears, like apples, contain good amounts of the soluble fiber pectin, known to help protect the body from environmental toxins that may affect fertility.

Pectin is a helpful regulator for bowel activity, a useful tool to support other body functions necessary for fertility. Because it attracts toxins that enter the body through food and also binds to those being eliminated through the liver, it may help prevent toxic metals, such as mercury and lead, from entering the blood circulation, where they can affect the reproductive system. Pectin is mildly diuretic and laxative, and works with insoluble fiber to clean out your bowels regularly. Healthy bowel function can help support correct female hormone balance and pectin also has prebiotic action; its fiber feeds our beneficial probiotic or healthy bowel bacteria, which help regulate levels of estrogen and progesterone to prepare for conception.

- The soluble fiber pectin removes toxins that may reduce the chances of conception.
- Pectin and insoluble fiber help regulate bowel function to further support detoxification.
- Pectin feeds healthy bacteria for the correct female hormone balance needed for fertility.

Practical tips:
You need to eat the skins of pears to benefit from the cleansing insoluble fiber. Eat like an apple, or stew them with some cinnamon. Pears are often included in diets for those with food sensitivities because they are known to be hypoallergenic.

DID YOU KNOW?

Pears make the perfect sweet snack, because the pectin they contain slows down the rate at which your body absorbs the sugars present in them. This is the opposite to the quick-fix sugars found in foods, such as cookies, which can contribute to highs and lows of energy and mood.

MAJOR NUTRIENTS PER MEDIUM-SIZE PEAR

Calories	58
Total fat	Trace
Protein	0.68 g
Carbohydrate	27.52 g
Fiber	5.5 g
Vitamin C	7.5 mg
Potassium	212 mg

Pear, beet, and spinach juice

SERVES 1

1 beet, trimmed, peeled,
   and chopped
1 pear, cored and chopped
1 cup fresh spinach leaves,
   plus one to decorate
filtered water, to taste

Method

1 Place the beet, pear, and spinach in a food processor or blender
and process. Dilute with filtered water to taste. Pour into a glass
and decorate with the spinach leaf. Serve immediately.

18

PASSION FRUIT

The name may refer to religious rather than sexual passion, but the rich antioxidant status of this fruit nonetheless renders it potent as a fertility boost.

With its high levels of antioxidant vitamin C, vitamin A, and beta-carotene, including passion fruit in your diet can help protect you against the day-to-day damage caused by environmental factors that can harm sperm and eggs. Vitamin C is water soluble and so protects watery areas of the body between and inside cells, as well as improving sperm count and quality. Vitamin A and beta-carotene are fat soluble, which means they protect the fat-rich testes and semen, and the cell walls of the egg and womb. Antioxidants also stop the male immune system from destroying its own sperm, and the fiber in passion fruit sweeps harmful toxins out of the body via the digestive system.

- Vitamin C protects all cells from environmental harm and improves sperm count and quality.
- Vitamin A and beta-carotene protect the testes, womb, and egg from damage.
- All of the above antioxidants prevent the male immune system from attacking its own sperm.
- High fiber removes toxins that increase the risk of infertility.

Practical tips:
Choose passion fruit that looks wrinkled because this means the fruit has ripened. Keep in the refrigerator for up to a week. The pulp and juice with seeds removed are most often used as flavoring, and are a healthy way to sweeten yogurts and top fruit salads.

DID YOU KNOW?

Its name and South American roots give passion fruit sexy connotations, and it is often served as an aphrodisiac in cocktail form. However, the alcoholic content of these drinks makes them difficult to recommend as a fertility treatment.

MAJOR NUTRIENTS PER MEDIUM-SIZE PASSION FRUIT

Calories	17
Total fat	0.13 g
Protein	0.4 g
Carbohydrate	4.21 g
Fiber	1.9 g
Vitamin C	5.4 mg
Vitamin A	229 IU
Beta-carotene	134 mcg
Potassium	63 mg

Salmon with passion fruit salsa

SERVES 4 (G) (A) (Q)

4 salmon steaks, about 6 oz each
finely grated rind and juice of 1 lime
  or ½ lemon
pepper

Passion fruit salsa

1 large mango, peeled,
  pitted, and diced
1 red onion, finely chopped
2 passion fruit
2 fresh basil sprigs
2 tbsp lime juice

Method

1 Rinse the salmon steaks under cold running water, pat dry with paper towels, and place in a large, shallow, nonmetallic dish. Sprinkle with the lime rind and pour the juice over them. Season to taste with pepper, cover, and let stand while you make the passion fruit salsa.

2 Place the mango flesh in a bowl with the onion. Cut the passion fruit in half and scoop out the seeds and pulp with a teaspoon into the bowl. Tear the basil leaves and add them to the bowl with the lime juice, then stir well. Cover with plastic wrap and reserve until needed.

3 Preheat the broiler to high. Cook the salmon steaks under the broiler for 3–4 minutes on each side. Serve immediately with the salsa.

19

GREEN TEA

The antioxidant compound epigallocatechin gallate (EGCG) found in green tea is able to move inside cells and help protect our DNA from damage.

This is vital in terms of reproduction because our DNA determines the way in which we replicate cells. It is believed that the tea's active compounds, including EGCG, other similar catechins, and hypoxanthine, may help the fertilization of oocytes, or egg cells, and create more embryos that are able to mature. Another bioflavonoid (plant chemical) in green tea is quercetin, which helps improve semen quality and aids circulation, bringing blood flow to the sexual organs. Prepare for pregnancy, and increase the chances of it, by switching from regular tea and coffee in advance so that you avoid caffeine withdrawal when pregnant.

- High in antioxidants, such as EGCG, which protect DNA from damage and enable cell replication.
- These compounds may also help fertilization of the egg to occur and embryos to grow.
- A healthy, low caffeine source that helps wean prospective mothers off tea and coffee in preparation for pregnancy.

DID YOU KNOW?

Some studies have suggested that drinking more than half a cup of green tea daily may actually double a woman's chances of conceiving, due to the tea's high antioxidant content.

MAJOR NUTRIENTS PER 225 ml/ABOUT 1 CUP GREEN TEA

Calories – approx*	2
Total fat	0 g
Protein	0 g
Carbohydrate	0 g
Fiber	0 g
Catechins*	3.75 g

* can vary greatly between varieties and strength of brew

Practical tips:

Green tea, which contains about 5 mg of caffeine per cup, is made by drying the leaves of the plant Camellia sinensis. Black, "normal" tea comes from the same plant but is fermented and much higher in caffeine, at about 50 mg a cup. Drink green tea in moderation when pregnant and don't let it brew for more than a minute; this will ensure the caffeine content is low and the taste is not too bitter.

Spiced poached pears in green tea

SERVES 2 (A) (V) (Q)

2 slightly underripe pears,
   halved and peeled

1 tsp lemon juice

3½ cups water

4 slices fresh ginger

2 star anise

1 cinnamon stick

1 tbsp honey

2 green tea bags

Method

1 Using a melon baller or teaspoon, scoop out the core of each
pear. Squeeze the lemon juice over the pears to prevent them
from browning.

2 Bring the water to a boil in a large sauté pan. Reduce the heat to
a simmer and add the ginger, star anise, cinnamon, and honey.
Stir until the honey melts, then add the pears.

3 Simmer the pears for 15–20 minutes, partially covered, until tender,
then remove from the pan, using a slotted spoon. Increase the
heat slightly, add the green tea, and simmer for about 5 minutes,
until the cooking liquid has reduced and become syrupy.

4 Remove the spices and tea bags from the cooking syrup. Serve
2 pear halves per person with the syrup spooned over the top.

20 BRAZIL NUTS

Brazil nuts are excellent sources of selenium, zinc, and vitamin E, which work together to produce good-quality sperm and protect the egg from damage.

Brazil nuts are fantastic packages of protein, fiber, complex carbohydrates, and healthy fatty acids. Each one of the nutritional elements they offer is needed for reproduction. Vitamin B6, zinc, and magnesium contribute to the production of sex hormones, while healthy zinc and folate (folic acid) levels are essential for upcoming fetal development. Brazil nuts contain balanced levels of the minerals calcium and magnesium, too, which are excellent for bone growth; as "calming minerals," they can also help reduce anxiety that can increase the risk of infertility.

- Contain high antioxidant levels, promoting healthy, intact sperm and egg.
- Each nut is nature's fertility package of fiber, fatty acids, carbohydrates, protein, vitamins, and minerals.
- Vitamin B6, zinc, and magnesium enable healthy sex hormone balance.
- Zinc and folate support the embryo as it matures.
- Contain balanced calcium and magnesium to support mother and baby bone health and reduce stress.

Practical tips:
Brazil nuts have a pleasant, creamy taste that makes them a perfect snack or protein addition to cereals, or fruit and yogurt. Like all nuts and seeds, their essential fatty acid content is easily damaged by heat and light, so they should not be cooked.

DID YOU KNOW?

Organic Brazil nuts contain much higher amounts of selenium than nonorganic nuts. You should also choose unshelled instead of shelled for the same reason.

MAJOR NUTRIENTS PER 25 G/ABOUT 5 SHELLED NUTS

Calories	197
Total fat	19.9 g
Omega-6 fatty acids	6,169 mg
Protein	4.3 g
Carbohydrate	3.7 g
Fiber	23 g
Vitamin B3	0.06 mg
Vitamin B6	0.30 mg
Vitamin E	1.72 mg
Folate	7 mcg
Calcium	48 mg
Magnesium	113 mg
Zinc	1.2 mg
Selenium	575 mcg

Oat and nut crunch mix

SERVES 8   (G) (A) (V) (Q)

olive oil, for brushing
1 cup rolled oats
3 tbsp pine nuts
⅓ cup pistachio nuts
   or hazelnuts
¼ cup almonds
8 coarsely chopped Brazil nuts
2 tbsp sunflower seeds
2 tbsp pumpkin seeds
⅓ cup chopped dried
   plumped apricots
¼ cup golden raisins
1 tsp ground cinnamon

Method

1 Heat a nonstick skillet over medium heat and brush with a little oil.
   Add the oats and pine nuts and cook, stirring continuously, for
   8–10 minutes, or until they smell nutty and look a little golden.
   Let stand to cool.

2 Transfer the toasted oat mixture to a large bowl and add all the
   remaining ingredients, then mix together well. Use as a topping
   for yogurt or fruit. It will keep for up to 2 weeks in the refrigerator.

First Trimester

Congratulations! You may be feeling changes to your body already. For many women, the first three months of pregnancy can be the hardest, with fatigue and morning sickness most likely to strike now. Being careful about what you eat can help, by ensuring steady blood-sugar levels, and providing the nutrients—such as the B vitamins and iron—that may be depleted at this time. Folate (folic acid), vitamin E, and zinc support the growth of the baby and placenta.

Certain foods can help minimize common symptoms, the best-known being ginger for nausea. Foods that support immunity are also particularly important now, when it is naturally lowered to protect the embryo from being rejected by the mother's body. Those foods that promote detoxification and the elimination of harmful substances also protect your baby at this delicate stage.

(G) Growth of baby

(B) Brain development of baby

(A) Immunity-supporting antioxidants

(N) Natural remedy

(V) Suitable for vegetarians

(Q) Quick and easy to prepare

21 GINGER

Ginger has been used for thousands of years as a medicine for nausea and morning sickness. Its active compound gingerol also encourages good digestion.

Being able to eat healthy, nutritious food is vital during all stages of pregnancy, but this can be difficult in the early months when nausea is most likely. Ginger helps keep up the appetite by curbing nausea, and it also helps rectify any digestive disharmony that may be contributing to the problem. It is a powerful antimicrobial, which means that it kills off harmful bacteria, yeasts, and viruses that may harm the fetus. Its strong antioxidant action, derived from 12 different substances that together have a more protective effect than vitamin C, also protects the growing baby from damage.

- May help reduce morning sickness so that the mother-to-be can retain her natural appetite; supports the absorption of vital nutrients.
- Contains high antioxidant levels that protect the embryo from damage.
- Kills off harmful bacteria and so helps prevent illness during this crucial time.

Practical tips:
A quick morning sickness remedy is ginger syrup with sparkling water. Others swear by ginger tea. It is available in tea bags, but a few slices of fresh ginger with hot water is more potent. Ginger cookies may be useful in emergencies, although the added sugar may exacerbate the problem in the long run.

DID YOU KNOW?

Studies have shown ginger to be superior to the common antinausea medicine Dramamine. It is especially useful during pregnancy, when a natural substance is preferable to a medication.

MAJOR NUTRIENTS PER 15 G/ ABOUT 2½ TBSP FRESH GINGER

Calories	12
Total fat	0.11 g
Protein	0.27 g
Carbohydrate	2.66 g
Fiber	0.3 g
Vitamin C	2.4 mg
Potassium	62 mg

Gingered chicken and vegetable salad

SERVES 4 (A) (N)

4 scallions, chopped

1-inch piece fresh ginger,
    peeled and finely chopped

2 garlic cloves, crushed

3 tbsp vegetable oil

4 skinless, boneless chicken
    breasts, cut into 1-inch
    pieces

Vegetable salad

1 tbsp vegetable oil

1 onion, sliced

2 garlic cloves, chopped

8 baby corn, halved

1½ cups diagonally halved
    snow peas

1 red bell pepper, seeded
    and sliced

3-inch piece cucumber,
    peeled, seeded, and sliced

4 tbsp soy sauce

1 tbsp honey

few fresh Thai basil leaves

6 oz fine egg or buckwheat
    noodles

Method

1 Mix the scallions, ginger, garlic, and 2 tablespoons of the oil
   together in a shallow dish and add the chicken. Cover and marinate
   for at least 3 hours. Lift the meat out of the marinade and set aside.

2 Heat 1 tablespoon of the oil in a wok and stir-fry the onion for
   1–2 minutes. Add the garlic and the rest of the vegetables except
   the cucumber, and cook for 2–3 minutes, until just tender. Add the
   cucumber, half of the soy sauce, the honey, and basil, and mix gently.

3 Soak the noodles for 2–3 minutes, or prepare according to package
   directions, until tender, and drain. Sprinkle the remaining soy sauce
   over them and arrange on plates. Top with the cooked vegetables.

4 Add the remaining oil to the wok, and stir-fry the chicken over high
   heat for 6 minutes, until cooked through and golden. Arrange the
   chicken on top of the salad and serve hot or warm.

22 ROOIBOS TEA

Rooibos is refreshing and caffeine-free. It provides antioxidants to support immunity, which is lowered in early pregnancy to prevent rejection of the embryo.

A mother's natural immune suppression in early pregnancy prevents the growing baby from being attacked as a foreign body. Rooibos is very high in polyphenols—protective antioxidants, such as quercetin, rutin, and ferulic acid—that support circulation and help prevent allergies that can heighten immune reactions. Rooibos also contains the antioxidant enzyme superoxide dismutase, which protects the body's cells—including a developing fetus—from damage by oxygen. Rooibos isn't technically a tea because it isn't derived from the *Camellia sinensis* plant, but from a legume. This means that it is extremely low in the tannins present in "normal" tea, which can prevent the absorption of iron. Iron is vital in pregnancy because it supports blood flow to the growing baby.

- Rich antioxidant profile supports natural immunity, which becomes suppressed during pregnancy.
- These substances also support circulation and prevent allergies, so helping to prevent miscarriage.
- Low tannin content makes rooibos preferable to normal tea, because tannin in regular tea and coffee hinders iron absorption and can reduce blood flow to the baby.

Practical tips:
Drink with milk as "normal" tea, or with lemon or honey. Limit intake to 2–3 cups a day in total. Some rooibos tea blends are mixed with herbal products that should be avoided during pregnancy.

DID YOU KNOW?
Rooibos tea has been used for hundreds of years by the African Bushman, one of the world's oldest peoples, especially to treat nausea, stomach cramps, and constipation during pregnancy.

MAJOR NUTRIENTS PER 225 ml/ABOUT 1 CUP ROOIBOS TEA

Calories—approx*	2
Total fat	0 g
Protein	0 g
Carbohydrate	0 g
Fiber	0 g
Polyphenols*	60–80 mg

* can vary greatly between varieties and strength of brew

Spiced tea-soaked dried fruit salad

SERVES 4 (A)(N)(V)

⅔ cup dried apricots

8 dried apple rings

4 dried pears

⅔ cup golden raisins

⅓ cup dried cherries

2 rooibos tea bags

several strips freshly pared
   lemon peel

1 cinnamon stick

1 star anise

Greek-style yogurt and honey,
   to serve

Method

1 Put the dried fruit and the tea bags in a heatproof bowl and pour over enough boiling water to cover the fruit by 1 inch. Set aside and let the fruit stew in the water for at least 2 hours, but ideally overnight, stirring occasionally.

2 Transfer the fruit and any remaining soaking liquid, the lemon peel, cinnamon stick, and star anise into a saucepan over medium heat. If necessary, add extra water so the fruit is just covered and simmer for 10–20 minutes, until the fruit is plump and soft.

3 Remove the pan from the heat and let the fruit and liquid cool.

4 Spoon the fruit into bowls, top with yogurt and honey, and serve immediately.

23 AVOCADOS

The abundant oils and fiber in avocados help the liver to maintain healthy hormone levels. This supports the growing baby and helps prevent nausea.

Any fears about the fat content of avocados need to be discarded, especially during the first trimester of pregnancy. A growing baby needs these valuable oils to start developing, especially in fat-rich areas, such as the heart and brain. These oils carry with them fat-soluble nutrients, such as vitamins A and E, and the carotenoid lutein, which protect these delicate fatty areas from damage as they grow. The minerals calcium, magnesium, and potassium—avocados contain 60 percent more potassium than bananas—help support the mother's increasing metabolism and heart rate. They also help to regulate fluid balance and maintain healthy blood pressure. Although high blood pressure is unlikely to pose a problem at this point of the pregnancy, support from the beginning as a preventive measure is advised.

- Contain healthy fats that support liver health and the development of the baby's heart and brain.
- Fat-soluble nutrients, such as vitamins A and E, and lutein, protect these fatty body parts from damage.
- Calcium, magnesium, and potassium support the mother's increasing heart rate, metabolism, and blood pressure.

Practical tips:
Avocado can be a pleasing snack, even when morning sickness is an all-day problem, and it is a good choice if food intake is minimal. If solid food is off-putting, it can be made into a smoothie.

DID YOU KNOW?

Some people believe avocados to be the perfect natural food because they contain everything a person—and, therefore, a growing baby—needs to survive.

MAJOR NUTRIENTS PER MEDIUM-SIZE AVOCADO

Calories	322
Total fat	29.47 g
Monounsaturated fat	19.7 g
Polyunsaturated fat	3.65 g
Protein	4.02 g
Carbohydrate	17.15 g
Fiber	13.5 g
Vitamin A	293 IU
Vitamin E	4.16 mg
Potassium	975 mg
Magnesium	58 mg
Calcium	24 mg
Lutein/Zeaxanthin	545 mcg

Avocado power pack

SERVES 1–2 Ⓖ Ⓑ Ⓐ Ⓥ Ⓠ

1 pear, peeled, cored, and sliced

1½ cups baby leaf spinach

4 fresh parsley sprigs

¼ cucumber

½ ripe avocado, pitted and peeled

½ tsp spirulina powder (available from healthfood stores)

1 Brazil nut, coarsely chopped

Method

1 Put the pear, spinach, parsley, cucumber, and avocado into a food processor or blender. Process until smooth, then pour into a glass.

2 Mix the spirulina powder with just enough water to make a thick liquid, then swirl into the juice. Sprinkle the Brazil nut over, then serve.

24 WALNUT OIL

Walnut oil provides a great balance of fatty acids during the first trimester, at a time when the baby's nervous system is undergoing intense development.

The omega-6 fatty acids in walnut oil help the body to maintain a healthy balance between sex hormones, which lowers the risk of miscarriage. Walnut oil also contains useful levels of omega-3 fatty acids, needed to support a baby's developing brain and spinal cord. These omega-3 fatty acids, along with omega-9 fatty acids (oleic acid), support the baby's heart development, too. During this crucial time, when a healthy immune system is vital to ward off infections, walnut oil also offers high levels of the antioxidant substances ellagic acid and phytosterols. These help the liver eliminate toxins that can pose a danger to your pregnancy by damaging cells and increasing the chances of inflammation and infection.

- Omega-6 fatty acids balance the sex hormones, while omega-3 fatty acids support brain development.
- Omega-3 and omega-9 fatty acids help create a healthy heart and keep problematic inflammation at bay.
- Ellagic acid and phytosterols fight against toxins and infections that can increase the risk of miscarriage.

Practical tips:
Store walnut oil in dark glass bottles; the fatty acids it contains can absorb hormone-disrupting chemicals from plastic. It should also be stored away from heat and light. Heating walnut oil can create damaging trans fats, so save it for salad dressings and smoothies. Choose cold-pressed types and avoid roasted or toasted oils.

DID YOU KNOW?

Walnut oil contains melatonin, a substance our brains use as a hormone to regulate sleep patterns, which can be affected from very early pregnancy. It also protects genetic material, including DNA, from damage.

MAJOR NUTRIENTS PER 15 ml/1 tbsp WALNUT OIL

Calories	120
Total fat	13.6 g
Monounsaturated fat	3.1 g
Omega-3 fatty acids	1404 mg
Omega-6 fatty acids	7141 mg
Omega-9 fatty acids	2997 mg
Vitamin E	0.1 mg
Phytosterols	23.8 mg

Roasted winter salad with walnut oil dressing

SERVES 2 (B)(A)(V)

1 parsnip, cut into batons
3 cups peeled and seeded, bite-
*   size butternut squash pieces*
1 uncooked beet, halved and cut
*   into wedges*
1 large onion, cut into wedges
1 tbsp olive oil
2 large garlic cloves, unpeeled

Dressing
2 tbsp walnut oil
2 tsp cider vinegar
½ tsp honey
1 tsp wholegrain mustard
pepper
1 tsp warm water

Method

1 Preheat the oven to 400°F. Toss the parsnip, squash, beet, and onion in the olive oil and arrange in a single layer in a large roasting pan. Add the garlic and roast, turning once, for 30–35 minutes, until tender.

2 Meanwhile, to make the dressing, mix together the walnut oil, vinegar, honey, mustard, and pepper with the water.

3 When the vegetables and garlic are ready, transfer the vegetables to a serving dish and squeeze the garlic onto a plate. Mash the garlic with the back of a fork, then stir into the dressing. Pour the dressing over the vegetables and serve warm or at room temperature.

25 POMEGRANATE

Pomegranate juice has been found to contain around three times the protective dose of antioxidant polyphenols of either red wine or green tea.

The polyphenols in the fruit help to increase the circulation, keeping a growing baby supplied with vital blood and oxygen. This may reduce the negative effects on the brain that a baby born before 34 weeks risks, because it is starved of a steady flow of blood and oxygen. It will also provide a healthy dose of vitamin C and folate (folic acid) to encourage all growth and development. Pomegranate juice has been found to help problems associated with high altitude in pregnant women, such as air travel, which may be part of an expectant mother's life during these early stages. High potassium helps this effect by aiding hydration.

- Rich polyphenols help blood and oxygen flow to the baby's brain and may reduce the risk of damage if born prematurely.
- Contains vitamin C and folate, which support all growth processes.
- Pomegranate juice has been shown to help reduce the negative effects of flying, while potassium assists hydration.

Practical tips:
Pomegranate juice has risen in popularity in the last few years and is now widely available. It is high in sugar, however, so limit consumption to a few glasses a day and dilute by up to half with water. It is even better to eat the fruit because you will also get the benefit of the cleansing fiber. Avoid pomegranate seed extract during pregnancy, because it can stimulate uterine contractions.

DID YOU KNOW?

Pomegranates were the primary symbol of Aphrodite, the Greek goddess of love who gave her name to "aphrodisiac." In Iran, these wonder fruits are recommended to pregnant women for their iron content.

MAJOR NUTRIENTS PER MEDIUM-SIZE POMEGRANATE

Calories	234
Total fat	3.3 g
Protein	4.71 g
Carbohydrate	52.73 g
Fiber	11.3 g
Vitamin C	28.8 mg
Folate	107 mcg
Calcium	28 mg
Magnesium	34 mg
Potassium	666 mg
Iron	0.85 mg
Selenium	1.4 mcg

Chicken with pomegranate salsa

SERVES 2

2 skinless, boneless chicken
    breasts, about 6 oz each
1 tbsp olive oil
salad greens, to serve
salt and pepper

Pomegranate salsa

1 small avocado
1 tbsp diced red onion
1-inch piece cucumber, seeded
    and diced
juice of ½ lime
2 tbsp chopped fresh cilantro
¼ cup pomegranate seeds

Method

1 Flatten the chicken breasts with a meat mallet or the end of a rolling pin. Heat a ridged grill pan, brush the chicken with oil, season with salt and pepper, then grill for about 6 minutes over medium–high heat, turning once, until blackened in places and cooked through.

2 Halve the avocado, pry out the pit, then peel away the skin. Cut the avocado into small chunks and place in a bowl with the red onion, cucumber, lime juice, cilantro, and pomegranate seeds. Season with pepper and stir gently until combined.

3 Serve the chicken with salad greens and a spoonful of the pomegranate salsa.

26 CELERY

Eating celery is one of the easiest ways to help bring down high blood pressure, which reduces the risk of later developing serious complications, including preeclampsia.

Celery contains two substances, apigenin and phthalide, which widen blood vessels, and three minerals, potassium, calcium, and magnesium, which relax them. The combined effect is to keep blood pressure at a healthy level. Celery also contains the calming amino acid tryptophan, from which we make the sleep and mood neurotransmitter serotonin, so it helps to minimize the stress and anxiety that can contribute to miscarriage risk. Its folate (folic acid) content helps prevent birth defects, and the high potassium and water content help prevent dehydration and keep fluid available to the embryo. A mother-to-be can draw energy from the vitamin C, B vitamins, and magnesium, making it less likely that she will turn to sugary snacks.

- Apigenin, phthalide, tryptophan, potassium, calcium, and magnesium maintain healthy blood pressure and reduce stress.
- Contains folate for healthy fetal development.
- High potassium and water content ensures hydration of the mother and extra fluid for the embryo.
- Vitamin C, the B vitamins, and magnesium all balance blood sugar levels, promoting sustained energy.

Practical tips:
Celery is one of the simplest snacks—just munch on a stalk or, for extra protein, dip some into hummus or a bean dip. It is an ideal bedtime nibble for people who find sleep difficult.

DID YOU KNOW?

Celery has a long history as a remedy for anxiety, high blood pressure, and sleep problems, all of which can be experienced by women in pregnancy.

MAJOR NUTRIENTS PER 100 G/ABOUT 1 CUP CHOPPED CELERY

Calories	16
Total fat	0.17 g
Protein	0.69 g
Carbohydrate	2.97 g
Fiber	1.6 g
Vitamin C	3.1 mg
Vitamin B3	0.32 mg
Vitamin B5	0.25 mg
Folate	36 mcg
Calcium	40 mg
Magnesium	11 mg
Potassium	260 mg

Gazpacho with celery salsa

SERMES 2   (G) (A) (N) (V)

*2 slices day-old spelt bread, crusts
   removed*

½ cup water, for soaking

4 tomatoes, seeded and skinned

*1 small cucumber, peeled, seeded,
   and chopped*

*1 red bell pepper, seeded and
   chopped*

*1 large red chile, seeded and
   finely chopped*

1 large garlic clove

3 tbsp olive oil

juice of 1 lemon

pepper

Celery salsa

1 celery stalk, sliced

*1 small avocado, peeled, pitted,
   and diced*

6 large basil leaves

Method

1 Soak one of the slices of bread in the water for 5 minutes.

2 Put the bread, tomatoes and their juices, cucumber, red bell pepper,
   three-quarters of the chile, the garlic, 1 tablespoon of the oil, and
   the lemon juice (reserving 1 teaspoon) in a food processor or
   blender and process until combined but still a little chunky. Season
   with pepper, then chill for 2–3 hours.

3 Just before serving, make the celery salsa. Put the celery, avocado,
   reserved lemon juice, basil, and remaining chile in a bowl, and stir
   until combined.

4 Cut the second slice of bread into cubes. Heat the remaining olive
   oil in a skillet and fry the bread for about 5 minutes, or until golden
   and crisp.

5 Ladle the soup into bowls and top with a large spoonful of the salsa
   and the croutons.

27

SUNFLOWER SEEDS

Sunflower seeds contain healthy doses of three key nutrients—folate, vitamin E, and zinc. A developing baby needs each of these in order to develop and grow.

During the first 12 weeks, when the embryo is developing, nutrient-rich foods, such as sunflower seeds, support both the baby and the growing placenta. Vitamin E and folate (folic acid) help prepare the placenta's connection in the womb, ready for it to take over and sustain the pregnancy. They are also needed to develop the red blood cells that supply the placenta and baby with nutrients and oxygen, which they both need continually in order to flourish. The iron in sunflower seeds makes hemoglobin, the substance in blood that transports oxygen to where it is needed. Meanwhile, vitamin E and magnesium keep the mother's muscles intact so that her body is able to support the growing baby and recover after birth. Selenium and zinc enable the body to create antioxidant enzymes that protect the baby from damage.

- Folate, vitamin E, and zinc support growth of the baby and placenta.
- Vitamin E is needed to secure the placental link, and, in combination with iron, safeguards the oxygen supply to the baby.
- Vitamin E and magnesium content maintains muscle health to support the baby and the mother after the pregnancy.
- Contain selenium and zinc to protect the embryo from toxins.

DID YOU KNOW?

Increasing your protein intake during pregnancy can easily be achieved if you consume nuts and seeds, such as sunflower seeds, as well as meat, fish, eggs, dairy, beans, and whole grains.

MAJOR NUTRIENTS PER 15 G/ ABOUT 2 TBSP SUNFLOWER SEEDS

Calories	88
Total fat	7.72 g
Monounsaturated fat	2.78 g
Omega-6 fatty acids	3,457.2 mg
Omega-9 fatty acids	2,756.5 mg
Protein	3.12 g
Carbohydrate	3 g
Fiber	1.3 g
Vitamin E	5.28 mg
Folate	34 mcg
Magnesium	49 mg
Potassium	97 mg
Phosphorus	99 mg
Iron	0.79 mg
Selenium	7.9 mcg
Zinc	0.75 mg

Practical tips:
Store in an airtight glass jar in a cupboard. The fatty acids are easily damaged, which can potentially be harmful, so avoid toasting. Sprinkle on salads, in cereals, and on oatmeal.

Apricot, oat, and sunflower seed bars

MAKES 12 (G) (B) (A) (V)

¾ cup rolled oats

¼ cup dried flaked coconut

¼ cup sunflower seeds

1¾ cups coarsely chopped
   plumped dried apricots

½ cup raisins

½ cup fresh orange juice

¼ cup slivered almonds

Method

1 Put the oats in a dry skillet and toast for 5 minutes over medium–low heat, tossing the skillet regularly, until beginning to turn golden. Remove from the skillet and let cool.

2 Put the coconut in the skillet and toast, tossing it regularly, for 2 minutes, until light golden. Let cool.

3 Put the oats and sunflower seeds in a food processor or blender. Process until coarsely chopped, then put in a bowl.

4 Put the apricots, raisins, and orange juice in the food processor or blender and process to a thick puree. Spoon the fruit puree into the bowl with the oat mixture. Add the toasted coconut and slivered almonds, and stir until combined into a thick paste.

5 Line a 10 x 7-inch pan with rice paper or parchment paper. Transfer the fruit mixture to the pan and, using a palette knife, spread into an even layer about ½ inch thick. Chill for about 1 hour in the refrigerator until firm, then slice into 12 pieces.

28 RASPBERRIES

Raspberries are a delicious way for a mother-to-be to load up on antioxidants that will protect the developing baby and keep it supplied with vital oxygen.

Raspberries are one of the most abundant sources of antioxidants in the plant kingdom. Their ample supply of vitamin C, quercetin, and proanthocyanidins helps prevent harmful free radicals (unstable molecules) from damaging the susceptible new tissues of a developing baby. These three also support the circulation so that it can deliver oxygen and nutrients effectively. Vitamin C is water soluble, which means it keeps watery areas between and inside cells free from harmful toxins, as well as the amniotic fluid that surrounds and protects the baby. The high fiber of raspberries—at 20 percent, they have one of the highest fiber levels of any fruit—takes a clean sweep of the body, moving out what is unwanted. Another good reason to include raspberries in the diet from early on is that they contain fragine, a chemical thought to strengthen the uterus, which will stand a mother in good stead when having birthing contractions later.

- Contain extremely high levels of antioxidants, which keep toxins from harming the baby, and help nourish it with oxygen and nutrients.
- High fiber content carries unwanted products out of the body.
- The substance fragine helps prepare the body for labor by strengthening the smooth muscle of the uterus.

Practical tips:
Raspberries are safe to eat at any time during pregnancy. A handful of raspberries enjoyed daily as a snack or with cereal, yogurt, or a smoothie is a safe way to support constant detoxification.

DID YOU KNOW?
Raspberries are the richest dietary source of ellagic acid, which helps the liver eliminate toxins and may also alleviate morning sickness.

MAJOR NUTRIENTS PER 100 G/ABOUT ¾ CUP RASPBERRIES

Calories	52
Total fat	0.65 g
Protein	1.2 g
Carbohydrate	11.94 g
Fiber	6.5 g
Vitamin C	26.2 mg
Potassium	151 mg
Lutein	136 mcg

Raspberry and apple smoothie

SERVES 1 (A)(V)(Q)

1 apple, peeled, cored, and
    chopped
2 tbsp chilled mineral water
½ cup fresh or thawed frozen
    raspberries
1 tsp honey (optional)
4 tbsp plain yogurt with live cultures
ice cubes

Method

1 Put the apple in a food processor or blender with the mineral water
   and process for 1 minute.
2 Reserve 2–3 raspberries for decoration and add the rest to the
   blender. Process for 30 seconds before adding the honey, if using,
   and then add the yogurt. Process for an additional minute.
3 Place a few ice cubes into a glass, pour over the smoothie,
   decorate with the reserved raspberries, and serve.

29 OATS

Oats provide a powerful combination of complex carbohydrates, ensuring a sustained release of energy at a time when the metabolic rate is increasing.

Oats and other slow-release foods balance your blood sugar by preventing sudden surges of sugar into the bloodstream. This keeps energy levels stable, helping to regulate appetite and prevent nausea, and keeps cravings for unhealthy foods at bay. The magnesium and zinc in oats also helps to keep blood sugar on an even keel by supporting the production of insulin, as well as the hormones estrogen and progesterone. At the same time, zinc, vitamin E, calcium, iron, and folate (folic acid) work together to support the baby's growth and development. Oats also help to keep bowel movements regular; constipation is a common pregnancy symptom and needs addressing to ensure that the mother is able to eliminate harmful toxins and maintain a healthy hormone balance.

- Slow-release energy food that regulates blood sugar, preventing sugar cravings and helping to prevent morning sickness.
- Contain magnesium and zinc, needed to support the hormones that balance blood sugar and maintain pregnancy.
- Zinc, vitamin E, calcium, iron, and folate are all necessary for fetal development.
- Help prevent constipation and remove toxins.

DID YOU KNOW?

Oats contain beta-glucans, chemicals that have positive effects on your immune system and which may, therefore, reduce the risk of early rejection of the growing embryo.

MAJOR NUTRIENTS PER 60 G/ABOUT ⅔ CUP OATS, UNCOOKED

Calories	233
Total fat	4 g
Protein	10 g
Carbohydrate	40 g
Fiber	6.4 g
Folate	34 mcg
Vitamin E	1.5 mg
Calcium	32 mg
Magnesium	106 mg
Potassium	257 mg
Zinc	2.4 mg
Iron	2.8 mg

Practical tips:

Cooked oats in oatmeals are much easier to digest than the raw flakes found in muesli or granola. You can soak oats overnight in water or apple juice to increase their ability to relieve constipation.

··

Apple and spice oatmeal

··

SERVES 4 Ⓖ Ⓐ Ⓝ Ⓥ Ⓠ

2½ cups milk or water
1¼ cups rolled oats
2 large apples, halved, cored,
  and grated
½ tsp ground allspice
honey, to serve (optional)

Method

1 Put the milk in a saucepan and bring to a boil. Sprinkle in the oats, stirring continuously. Reduce the heat to low and let the oats simmer for 10 minutes, stirring occasionally.

2 When the oatmeal is creamy and much of the liquid has evaporated, stir in the grated apple and allspice. Spoon into bowls and drizzle with the honey, if using.

30 EGGPLANT

The eggplant provides a wide spread of the nutrients that work together to support a healthy pregnancy, including antioxidants that help protect a baby from toxic damage.

The chlorogenic acid found in an eggplant is a powerful antioxidant. It also helps regulate blood sugar levels, promoting sustained energy levels, and assists our metabolism by reducing our body's uptake of sugar. Vitamins B3 and B5, zinc, and manganese also help the body release the most energy possible from the food we eat, thereby reducing sugar cravings. Nasunin is another antioxidant in eggplant, which particularly protects fatty areas, such as the baby's growing heart, brain, liver, and kidneys. Copper is a trace mineral needed for collagen production, the protein from which all human tissue is derived, and which is needed constantly to ensure the baby's continued development. The potassium in eggplant helps to keep blood pressure at a safe level.

- Chlorogenic acid protects the baby's cells from damage and regulates energy.
- Vitamins B3 and B5, zinc, and manganese help energy to be unlocked from food, ensuring a baby's growth.
- Nasunin prevents damage to fatty areas in the fetus.
- Contains copper, needed to make collagen for the baby to grow.
- Potassium ensures blood pressure stays within healthy parameters.

Practical tips:
It is recommended that everyone avoid salt beyond a little culinary seasoning whether pregnant or not, so instead of salting eggplants before cooking, try brushing slices with olive oil and broiling.

DID YOU KNOW?

Eggplant makes up part of the typical Mediterranean diet, which has been shown to have a positive effect on both the health of the mother and the child during pregnancy, resulting in a lower incidence of miscarriage and birth defects.

MAJOR NUTRIENTS PER 100 G/ ABOUT 1¼ CUPS DICED EGGPLANT

Calories	24
Total fat	0.19 g
Protein	1.01 g
Carbohydrate	5.7 g
Fiber	3.4 g
Vitamin B3	0.65 mg
Vitamin B5	0.28 mg
Zinc	0.16 mg
Copper	0.08 mg
Manganese	0.25 mg
Potassium	230 mg

Eggplant and tomatoes with capers

SERVES 2   (G)(B)(A)(V)(Q)

1 medium eggplant, cut into large,
    bite-size pieces

3 tbsp olive oil

1 onion, chopped

3 garlic cloves, chopped

1 celery stalk, thinly sliced

14 oz of canned plum tomatoes
    (1¾ cups)

1 tsp red wine vinegar

½ tsp sugar

2 tbsp capers, drained and rinsed

pepper

4 fresh basil sprigs, leaves torn,
    to garnish

Method

1 Steam the eggplant for 10 minutes, until tender.

2 Meanwhile, heat the oil in a saucepan and sauté the onion for 5 minutes, until softened. Add the garlic and celery and cook for another 5 minutes.

3 Add the tomatoes to the pan and break them down using the back of a spatula. Stir in the red wine vinegar, sugar, capers, and eggplant, then bring to a boil. Reduce the heat and simmer, partly covered, for 10 minutes, until reduced and thickened.

4 Season with pepper, then divide between two bowls and scatter over the basil to serve.

31 APPLES

Eating an apple can satisfy a sweet craving, helping to support changing demands on energy and a developing appetite, while sustaining blood sugar levels.

Regulating blood sugar levels to avoid highs and lows is the most fundamental way to control appetite, which can increase or decrease during the early stages of pregnancy. Keeping something in the stomach at all times can help keep nausea at bay, and choosing an apple may stop an expectant mother from reaching for unhealthy foods, such as cookies and caffeine. It is high levels of the fiber pectin that makes the release of sugar in apples so slow. The pectin also holds onto toxins in the bowel so that they can be safely removed from the body and the baby. The antioxidant quercetin in apples supports immunity at a time when it is naturally low and encourages blood flow, taking oxygen and nutrients to the womb.

• Apples naturally regulate blood sugar levels to correct appetite, reduce cravings for caffeine and sugar, and help prevent nausea.
• Pectin removes harmful toxins from the body.
• Quercetin's antioxidant action supports immunity and circulation.

Practical tips:
Nonorganic apples are sprayed with more pesticides than other fruits, so choose organic to reduce the amount of toxins you take into your body. An apple a day is an easy way to keep your bowels regular, and you can also make applesauce with added plums, dried plums (prunes), or dried apricots if you need some extra help.

DID YOU KNOW?

Eating four or more apples a week during pregnancy may reduce the likelihood of childhood asthma in your baby. Studies have shown them to be the one common dietary factor in mothers whose children had the best airway development.

MAJOR NUTRIENTS PER MEDIUM-SIZE APPLE

Calories	95
Total fat	0.31 g
Protein	0.47 g
Carbohydrate	25.13 g
Fiber	4.4 g
Vitamin C	8.4 mg
Vitamin A	98 mg
Potassium	195 mg

Oaty apple and cinnamon muffins

MAKES 12 (A) (N) (V)

oil or melted butter, for greasing
  (if using)
1⅔ cups whole wheat flour
¾ cup rolled oats
2 tsp baking powder
⅓ cup packed light brown sugar
1 tsp ground cinnamon
2 extra-large eggs
1 cup milk
½ cup peanut oil
1 tsp vanilla extract
2 apples, cored and grated

Method

1 Preheat the oven to 350°F. Grease a 12-cup muffin pan or line with 12 muffin cups.

2 Sift together the flour, oats, and baking powder into a large bowl, adding any husks that remain. Stir in the sugar and cinnamon.

3 Lightly beat the eggs in a large bowl, then beat in the milk and oil. Make a well in the center of the dry ingredients and pour in the beaten liquid ingredients. Add the vanilla extract and stir gently until just combined; do not overmix.

4 Stir the apple into the batter. Spoon the batter into the prepared muffin pan. Bake in the preheated oven for 25–30 minutes, until risen, golden brown, and firm to the touch.

5 Let the muffins stand in the pan for 5 minutes, then serve warm or transfer to a wire rack and let cool.

32 MINT

Mint has a gently calming effect, making it useful in early pregnancy, when anxiety is common, while its stomach-soothing properties can alleviate morning sickness.

Mint is known mainly for its ability to soothe and relax the smooth muscle and lining of the digestive tract, helping to reduce stomach pains, nausea, and heartburn, commonly experienced by women in the first trimester of pregnancy. This helps to relieve stress in the abdomen and stomach that can result in tension in the rest of the body, even causing constipation and subsequent toxic accumulation. Cleverly, mint can destroy unwanted harmful bacteria before it enters the bloodstream and potentially affects the growing embryo, while at the same time supporting the digestive environment that enables good probiotic bacteria to flourish.

- May help calm the whole body, helping to relieve the anxiety that is common in early pregnancy.
- Soothes the stomach to help reduce nausea, indigestion, constipation, and stomach pains.
- Helps prevent harmful bacteria reaching the baby.

Practical tips:
Mint is sometimes contraindicated in pregnancy as a herb that can bring on uterine contractions in women susceptible to miscarriage. However, this only applies to high doses, as you might get in supplements or herbal medicines. In normal culinary use, such as a few cups of mint tea per day, or the fresh leaf added to a smoothie, dressing, or salad, mint is safe and beneficial.

DID YOU KNOW?

Using mint to relieve aches, pains, and anxieties during pregnancy goes back millennia to the ancient Greeks, who named it "mintha," after a mythological nymph who was turned into a plant by Persephone.

MAJOR NUTRIENTS PER 15 G/2½ TBSP MINT

Calories	7
Total fat	0 g
Protein	0.5 g
Carbohydrate	1.2 g
Fiber	1 g
Folate	16 mcg
Calcium	30 mg
Magnesium	9 mg
Potassium	69 mg
Iron	1.8 mg

Mint and cannellini bean dip

SERVES 6   (G) (A) (N) (V) (Q)

6 oz of canned cannellini beans,
*   rinsed and drained (⅔ cup)*
1 small garlic clove, crushed
1 bunch of scallions, coarsely
*   chopped*
handful fresh mint leaves
2 tbsp tahini
2 tbsp olive oil
1 tsp ground cumin
1 tsp ground coriander
lemon juice
pepper

Method

1 Put the cannellini beans into a bowl. Add the garlic, scallions, mint, tahini, and olive oil. Mash well until smooth. Stir in the cumin, coriander, and lemon juice.

2 Season to taste with pepper. Mix thoroughly, cover with plastic wrap, and set aside in a cool place, but not the refrigerator, for 30 minutes to let the flavors develop fully.

3 Spoon the dip into individual bowls and serve at room temperature.

33 LIVE YOGURT

Live yogurt retains the bacteria used to ferment the milk and has a long tradition of supporting immunity and reducing digestive problems.

The immune-supporting effects of live yogurt occur by increasing and protecting the probiotic beneficial bacteria that naturally colonizes our digestive tracts. This reduces inflammation and helps prevent intolerances and allergies. Yogurt also helps regulate digestion, reducing the incidence of diarrhea and, particularly in pregnancy, constipation that may be at the heart of other symptoms, such as nausea, heartburn, flatulence, and bloating. Any buildup of waste products in the intestines needs to be addressed at the start of pregnancy, because it can lower the body's immunity and its ability to rid itself of toxins. Yogurt is a complete protein and a vegetarian source of vitamin B12, which means it is well equipped to support the baby's developing brain and body.

- Supports beneficial bacteria for immunity and detoxification.
- Ensures good digestive function, helping relieve nausea, heartburn, gas, and bloating.
- Contains protein and vitamin B12, needed to form the baby's brain and body tissues.

Practical tips:
Live Greek-style yogurt can be easier to digest because it contains less lactose and more protein, and may help women with morning sickness feel fuller easily. Choose organic dairy products, if possible, to reduce your exposure to hormones and antibiotics.

DID YOU KNOW?

Yogurt isn't only for eating, but can also help to relieve vaginal thrush symptoms when used topically. Thrush is a common pregnancy complaint and a warning to cut down on sugar in the diet.

MAJOR NUTRIENTS PER 100 ml/about ½ cup PLAIN WHOLE YOGURT

Calories	61
Total fat	3.25 g
Protein	3.47 g
Carbohydrate	4.66 g
Vitamin A	99 IU
Vitamin B2	0.14 mg
Vitamin B5	0.39 mg
Vitamin B12	0.37 mcg
Choline	15.2 mg
Calcium	121 mg
Potassium	155 mg

Apricot and yogurt cups

SERVES 4–6 (G)(B)(A)(N)(V)(Q)

2½ cups plain yogurt with live
   cultures

few drops of almond extract

2–3 tsp honey, warmed

½ cup whole blanched almonds,
   thinly sliced

1½ cups coarsely chopped,
   plumped dried apricots

Method

1 Line a 12-cup muffin pan with small paper cupcake liners.

2 Spoon the yogurt into a mixing bowl, add the almond extract,
honey, almonds, and apricots and stir well.

3 Spoon the mixture into the paper liners and freeze for
1½–2 hours, or until just frozen. Serve immediately.

34 BLACK BEANS

All beans have antioxidant properties but black beans are particularly special. The purple proanthocyanidins they contain ensure good blood flow to the womb.

The antioxidant power of black beans is around ten times that of the equivalent weight of oranges, so a meal based on these will help keep a baby safe by supporting the mother's immunity. Black beans also supply a great dose of folate (folic acid), not only needed for the baby's neural tube to form in the first four weeks of pregnancy, but later on for the production of the entire nervous system, producing red blood cells and all new cell growth. Vitamin B1 aids these processes by helping the body produce the energy needed to make it all happen. The high levels of protein, calcium, magnesium, and potassium in black beans also help strengthen the mother's muscles as they prepare to accommodate the growing baby.

- High antioxidant levels protect the growing baby from harm and help safeguard the pregnancy.
- Folate and vitamin B1 play crucial roles as the baby's nervous system grows and the mother's blood volume increases.
- Protein, calcium, magnesium, and potassium prepare the stomach muscles to stretch and support the baby.

Practical tips:
There is little nutritional difference between dried or canned beans. Look for those without salt or additives. If cooking from dried, presoaking helps break down the fibers that can cause flatulence. Soak overnight or boil for two minutes, then let the beans stand, covered in the water, for two hours, before rinsing and draining.

DID YOU KNOW?

Nature provides combinations of nutrients that help regulate the body. The minerals in beans, for example, naturally maintain good blood pressure levels, which can be jeopardized in early pregnancy as blood volume begins to increase.

MAJOR NUTRIENTS PER 100 G/ABOUT ½ CUP DRIED BLACK BEANS

Calories	341
Total fat	1.42 g
Protein	21.6 g
Carbohydrate	62.36 g
Fiber	15.2 g
Vitamin B1	0.9 mg
Folate	444 mcg
Vitamin E	0.21 mg
Calcium	123 mg
Magnesium	171 mg
Potassium	1,483 mg
Zinc	3.65 mg

Mixed bean chili

SERVES 4–6   (G) (B) (A) (V) (Q)

2 tbsp olive oil

1 onion, chopped

2 garlic cloves, finely chopped

1 red chile, seeded and chopped

1 small red bell pepper, seeded and chopped

1 tsp ground cumin

1 tsp ground coriander

1 tsp dried thyme

2 tomatoes, seeded and chopped

⅔ cup dried red kidney beans, soaked overnight, drained and rinsed

⅔ cup dried black beans, soaked overnight, drained and rinsed

⅔ cup dried pinto beans, soaked overnight, drained and rinsed

⅔ cup vegetable stock

pepper

chopped fresh cilantro, to garnish

Method

1 Heat the oil in a large, heavy-bottom saucepan. Add the onion and cook over medium heat, stirring occasionally, for 5 minutes. Stir in the garlic, chile, and red bell pepper and cook for another 3 minutes. Add the cumin, coriander, and thyme and cook, stirring, for 1–2 minutes.

2 Add the tomatoes, drained beans, and stock and bring to a boil, then reduce the heat and simmer, partly covered, for 12 minutes, stirring occasionally.

3 Season with pepper, then ladle half into a bowl. Mash well with a potato masher, then return the mashed beans to the pan. Serve immediately, sprinkled with chopped fresh cilantro.

35 ALMONDS

Almonds contain high levels of vitamin E, which protects the baby's delicate fat cells and helps produce both mother and baby's increasing red blood cell numbers.

MAJOR NUTRIENTS PER 25 G/20 ALMONDS

Calories	174
Total fat	15 g
Monounsaturated fat	9.27 g
Omega-6 fatty acids	3,619 mg
Omega-9 fatty acids	9,182 mg
Protein	6.6 g
Carbohydrate	6 g
Fiber	3 g
Vitamin B3	1.01 mg
Vitamin B5	0.14 mg
Vitamin E	7.4 mg
Calcium	80 mg
Magnesium	80 mg
Potassium	211.5 mg
Phosphorus	145.2 mg
Zinc	1.51 mg
Phytosterols	42.9 mg

The omega-6 fatty acids, B vitamins, zinc, and magnesium in almonds not only help to regulate estrogen and progesterone, which is essential to maintain pregnancy and reduce the risk of miscarriage, but also help keep up the mother's energy, good mood, and positive outlook. The minerals calcium and magnesium are also present in a perfectly balanced ratio, helping to soothe muscle tension, maintain healthy blood pressure, and keep the mother's brain firing on all cylinders. In the first trimester, the baby is busy storing calcium, ready to build bone, and is taking this from its mother. If there is not enough calcium in the diet, the mother's personal stores will be the ones to be depleted, often resulting in tooth decay or increased risk of osteoporosis later in life.

- Vitamin E helps prevent inflammation and ensure immunity, protect fatty areas of the baby's body, and create red blood cells.
- Omega-6 fatty acids, the B vitamins, zinc, and magnesium regulate hormones, energy, and mood.
- Contain calcium and magnesium for healthy blood pressure, baby's bone growth, and topping up the mother's stores.

Practical tips:
As an easy, portable snack, almonds help prevent drops in blood sugar that can cause nausea, fatigue, and dizziness. For some women, snacking every four hours is the only way to reduce these symptoms. Eat them raw and store away from heat and light.

Almond nut butter

SERVES 10 (G)(A)(V)(Q)

1 cup blanched whole almonds
5 tbsp light olive oil
2 tsp fajita spice blend
pinch of sea salt

Method

1 Put the almonds and oil in a food processor or blender and process to a coarse paste.

2 Transfer the nut butter to a bowl, then stir in the spice mixture and salt. Cover and store in the refrigerator.

36 CHICKEN

Chicken is a dense source of protein, which will provide the building blocks for a baby's development and growth. Protein forms the basis of every part of the human body.

We also receive a good dose of iron when eating chicken. The iron in chicken, and other animal products, is the most easily absorbed by the body. We are then able to use it to make hemoglobin to transport oxygen and create energy. Fatigue in the first trimester can often signal low iron stores and should be discussed with a doctor. It is low levels of iron and its companion vitamin B6, also present in chicken, that most often contribute to morning sickness. As well as helping our utilization of iron, B6 regulates the hormone estrogen, which can contribute to nausea and even vomiting at this early stage when the hormone is peaking. The selenium in chicken helps eliminate toxic metals, such as mercury and lead, which can harm the fetus.

- Dense protein, which provides the building materials a baby needs for full development.
- Contains easily utilized iron with vitamin B6, helping the body to create energy and combat fatigue and morning sickness.
- Selenium helps detoxify toxic metals that are harmful to the fetus.

Practical tips:

A free-range chicken will have a higher protein-to-fat ratio than other birds because it has been active, and is more likely to have been fed more nutritious food. Organic is the best option during pregnancy, because the hormones and antibiotics present in nonorganic meat may interfere with a mother's own hormones and immunity.

DID YOU KNOW?

You may have seen hyaluronic acid in the ingredients lists of skin-care creams, because it plumps out the skin. It is naturally present in chicken and will help a growing baby to hold onto water, keeping it fully hydrated.

MAJOR NUTRIENTS PER 100 G/3½ OZ CHICKEN, SKIN REMOVED

Calories	114
Total fat	2.59 g
Saturated fat	0.57 g
Monounsaturated fat	0.76 g
Protein	21.23 g
Carbohydrate	0 g
Vitamin B3	10.43 mg
Vitamin B5	1.43 mg
Vitamin B6	0.75 mg
Selenium	32 mcg
Iron	0.37 mg

Chicken and barley stew

SERVES 4 Ⓖ Ⓑ Ⓐ

2 tbsp olive oil

8 small, skinless chicken thighs

2 cups chicken stock

½ cup pearl barley, rinsed
    and drained

8 oz small new potatoes, scrubbed
    and halved lengthwise

2 large carrots, peeled and sliced

1 leek, trimmed and sliced

2 shallots, sliced

1 tbsp tomato paste

1 bay leaf

1 zucchini, trimmed and sliced

2 tbsp chopped fresh flat-leaf
    parsley, plus extra sprigs
    to garnish

2 tbsp cornstarch

4 tbsp water

salt and pepper

Method

1 Heat the oil in a large saucepan over medium heat. Add the chicken and cook for 3 minutes, then turn over and cook for an additional 2 minutes. Add the stock, barley, potatoes, carrots, leek, shallots, tomato paste, and bay leaf. Bring to a boil, reduce the heat, and simmer for 30 minutes.

2 Add the zucchini and chopped parsley, cover the pan, and cook for an additional 20 minutes, or until the chicken is cooked through. Remove the bay leaf and discard.

3 In a separate bowl, mix the cornstarch with the water and stir into a smooth paste. Add to the stew and cook, stirring, over low heat for an additional 5 minutes. Season to taste with a little salt and pepper.

4 Remove from the heat, ladle into warm serving bowls, and garnish with sprigs of fresh parsley.

37

TILAPIA

Protein levels in tilapia are comparative to chicken, but this fish also has DHA, the omega-3 fatty acid responsible for brain development and function in babies.

The DHA (docosahexaenoic acid) in tilapia is necessary for the development of the central nervous system, eyes, and brain. Some studies have found a link between DHA intake in pregnancy and a baby's future cognitive development, although the evidence is not conclusive. A woman's daily DHA requirements are at least 200 mg and increase during pregnancy (the exact amount is as yet undecided). Tilapia also contains omega-6 fatty acids, which work alongside omega-3 fatty acids and help maintain hormone balance. Its vitamin D content is valuable, too, for the full and healthy development of the baby's skeleton. The choline in tilapia is a B vitamin that is needed for brain development.

- Contains protein and DHA to support fetal brain and nervous system development.
- DHA intake during pregnancy may have a positive effect on children's future cognitive function.
- Vitamin D is needed for healthy skeleton development.
- Choline is needed for brain development.

Practical tips:
Tilapia does not have an especially fishy taste or smell, and this can be helpful for women less inclined to eat fish, or who are put off the thought of it during early pregnancy. Broil, poach, or bake tilapia to get the most health benefits.

DID YOU KNOW?

Tilapia is low in the toxic metal mercury, which is known to contaminate tuna and swordfish and is especially harmful for pregnant women, increasing the risk of premature birth.

MAJOR NUTRIENTS PER 100 G/3½ oz FRESH TILAPIA

Calories	96
Total fat	1.7 g
Omega-3 fatty acids	220 mg
Omega-6 fatty acids	210 mg
Protein	20 g
Carbohydrate	0 g
Vitamin D	124 IU
Vitamin E	0.4 IU
Vitamin B3	3.9 mg
Vitamin B6	0.5 mg
Vitamin B12	1.58 mg
Folate	24 mcg
Choline	42.5 mg
Glutamic acid	3.21 g

Tilapia with watercress sauce

SERVES 4 (G) (B) (Q)

4 tilapia fillets, about
    6 oz each, skinned
juice of ½ lemon
5 tbsp olive oil
1 shallot, finely chopped
1 garlic clove, finely chopped
3 cups finely chopped watercress
1 cup crème fraîche, Greek yogurt,
    or sour cream
salt and pepper
watercress sprigs, to garnish
new potatoes, to serve

Method

1 Sprinkle the fish fillets with the lemon juice and season with pepper. Heat 3 tablespoons of the oil in a skillet. Add the fish and cook over medium–low heat for 3–4 minutes on each side.

2 Meanwhile, heat the remaining oil in a saucepan. Add the shallot and garlic and cook over low heat, stirring occasionally, for 5 minutes, until soft. Stir in the watercress and cook, stirring occasionally, for 2 minutes, until wilted. Stir in the crème fraîche, season to taste with a little salt and pepper, and heat gently.

3 Using a spatula, transfer the fish fillets to warm serving plates. Spoon the sauce over them, garnish with watercress sprigs, and serve immediately with new potatoes.

38

OLIVE OIL

The fat profile of olive oil is similar to human breast milk. As such, it can help to support a baby's growth throughout pregnancy, and beyond if the baby is breast-fed.

As one of the staples of the Mediterranean diet, olive oil is the oil to choose if you want to pass on the immune-enhancing properties of that diet—derived from substances including quercetin and oleic acid—to a developing child. The vitamin E in olive oil has been shown to be a supportive factor in the development of a baby's liver, kidneys, and pancreas, important if a baby is born prematurely. Thanks to the compound oleocanthal, which has the same anti-inflammatory action as ibuprofen, olive oil also helps to relieve those pregnancy aches and pains completely naturally.

- Contains healthy fats and immune-supporting chemicals, which can be passed on to a child even beyond pregnancy.
- Consumption during pregnancy has been shown to produce better breathing patterns in babies.
- Vitamin E helps reduce the risk of problems in the liver, kidneys, and pancreas in premature infants.
- Oleocanthal acts as a potent anti-inflammatory, so reducing aches and pains.

Practical tips:
Choose the best quality extra virgin, cold-pressed olive oil that you can afford and use it for salad dressings. Its high monounsaturated fat content means that it can be safely used when cooking at medium temperatures, such as when stir-frying or roasting.

DID YOU KNOW?

Olive oil is a fabulous natural moisturizer during early pregnancy. It will help prevent stretch marks later, and is free of the hormone-disrupting chemicals found in many commercial toiletries.

MAJOR NUTRIENTS PER 15 ml/1 TBSP OLIVE OIL

Calories	132
Total fat	15 g
Monounsaturated fat	4.62 g
Omega-6 fatty acids	1,464 mg
Omega-9 fatty acids	10,589 mg
Carbohydrate	0 g
Vitamin E	2.15 mg

Green pesto sauce

MAKES ½ CUP (G) (A) (N) (Q)

40 fresh basil leaves

3 garlic cloves, crushed

3 tbsp pine nuts

½ cup finely grated Parmesan
cheese

2–3 tbsp extra virgin olive oil

pepper

Method

1 Rinse the basil leaves and pat them dry with paper towels. Put
the basil leaves, garlic, pine nuts, and Parmesan into a food
processor or blender and process for 30 seconds, or until smooth.
Alternatively, pound all of the ingredients in a mortar with a pestle.

2 If you are using a food processor or blender, keep the motor running
and slowly add the olive oil. Alternatively, add the oil drop by drop
while stirring briskly. Season with pepper to taste.

39

PAPAYA

Papaya contains the digestive enzyme papain, which breaks down the proteins we eat, helping to reduce pregnancy heartburn, constipation, and nausea.

The hormone progesterone steadily rises in a mother's body during pregnancy, softening the muscles to let the womb expand. It can have the adverse effect of softening digestive muscles, resulting in heartburn, nausea, and constipation. The papain in papaya may help to correct this. The vitamin C in this fruit aids iron and calcium absorption. Vitamin C supports thyroid function, too, so promoting the development of a baby's brain and nervous system, and the production of collagen for structural growth. The carotenoids beta-carotene, lutein, and zeanxathin in papaya protect the embryonic fatty areas, such as the heart, brain, eyes, and skin, as they develop. Our bodies convert beta-carotene to vitamin A as it is required, helping us to avoid a harmful overload of this vitamin.

- Contains papain, which helps the body digest protein, reducing morning sickness, sluggish digestion, and heartburn.
- Vitamin C enables iron and calcium absorption, and supports thyroid function for brain development and collagen synthesis for skin, bone, and organs.
- Carotenoids protect the baby's growing fatty areas and produce vitamin A as it is needed for a healthy heart, brain, eyes, and skin.

Practical tips:
Include papaya in salads with fish or meat to break down these dense proteins. Do not take supplements while pregnant and avoid unripened papaya because it may cause uterine contractions.

DID YOU KNOW?

The rich colors of tropical fruit display their high carotenoid content. These antioxidants protect the fruit from UV damage from the sun as they ripen, just as they protect a growing baby's delicate body.

MAJOR NUTRIENTS PER MEDIUM-SIZE PAPAYA

Calories	120
Total fat	0.4 g
Protein	1.5 g
Carbohydrate	30 g
Fiber	5.5 g
Vitamin C	180 mg
Potassium	780 mg
Lutein/Zeanxathin	228 mcg
Beta-carotene	839 mcg

Papaya, avocado, and red bell pepper salad

SERVES 4–6   (G) (B) (A) (N) (V) (Q)

8 oz mixed salad greens

2–3 scallions, chopped

3–4 tbsp chopped fresh cilantro

1 small ripe papaya

2 red bell peppers, seeded, halved,
   and thinly sliced

1 avocado

1 tbsp lime juice

3–4 tbsp pumpkin seeds (optional)

Dressing

juice of 1 lime

large pinch of paprika

large pinch of ground cumin

1 garlic clove, finely chopped

4 tbsp extra virgin olive oil

Method

1 Combine the salad greens with the scallions and cilantro in
   a bowl. Mix well, then transfer the salad to a large serving dish.

2 Cut the papaya in half and scoop out the seeds with a spoon. Cut
   into quarters, remove the peel, and slice the flesh. Arrange on top of
   the salad greens. Add the bell peppers to the salad greens. Cut the
   avocado in half around the pit. Twist apart, then remove the pit with
   a knife. Carefully peel off the skin, dice the flesh, and toss in lime
   juice to prevent discoloration. Add to the other salad ingredients.

3 To make the dressing, whisk the lime juice, paprika, cumin, garlic,
   and oil together in a small bowl. Pour the dressing over the salad
   and toss lightly. Sprinkle with pumpkin seeds, if using.

40 ARUGULA

Like other members of the cabbage family, arugula contains sulforaphanes, chemicals that provide the optimum natural protection for a mother-to-be and a developing baby.

Sulforaphanes neutralize toxins and enable you to produce antioxidant enzymes in the liver that work over and over again long after eating. This far-reaching effect can prevent damage to both the baby's DNA and body parts in support of full and healthy development. It can also stimulate the other antioxidants you receive in your diet, thereby increasing their protective power. Arugula has dark leaves because it contains high levels of carotenoid antioxidants, and these together with the high vitamin C and E and folate (folic acid) content support the growth of tissues in the baby's developing body. The calcium in arugula is the main mineral for bone growth, ably assisted by vitamin C and beta-carotene. Meanwhile, potassium helps regulate body fluids to reduce puffiness and the risk of high blood pressure in pregnancy.

- Sulforaphanes provide long-term, natural antioxidant protection and rejuvenate other antioxidants so that they work at full power.
- Vitamins C and E and folate play interlinked roles in a baby's development.
- Contains calcium, vitamin C, and beta-carotene, which are all needed for skeleton building.
- Potassium helps prevent fluid retention and high blood pressure.

Practical tips:
The peppery taste of arugula leaves stimulates digestion, making them a healthy basis for any salad. Add to Italian dishes at the end of cooking, so they don't wilt. Wash thoroughly before use.

DID YOU KNOW?

Although full detoxification regimes are not advised during pregnancy because the released toxins could harm the baby, eating green leaves, such as arugula, naturally cleans out toxins on a safe, everyday basis.

MAJOR NUTRIENTS PER 15 G/ABOUT 1 CUP ARUGULA

Calories	4
Total fat	0 g
Protein	0.4 g
Carbohydrate	0.5 g
Fiber	0.2 g
Vitamin C	2.3 mg
Folate	15 mcg
Vitamin E	1.5 mg
Calcium	24 mg
Potassium	55 mg
Beta-carotene	214 mcg
Lutein/Zeaxanthin	533 mcg

Grilled shrimp with arugula and radicchio

SERVES 4 (G) (A) (Q)

1 garlic clove, crushed

juice of ½ lemon

4 tbsp extra virgin olive oil

¼ tsp dried chile flakes

8 oz large, shelled shrimp,
   without heads

8 radicchio leaves, sliced into
   ribbons

4 handfuls arugula

1 tsp balsamic vinegar

pepper

2 tbsp shredded fresh basil,
   to garnish

Method

1 Whisk the garlic and lemon juice with 3 tablespoons of the oil,
   the chile flakes, and pepper to taste. Pour over the shrimp and
   let marinate for 30 minutes.

2 Put the radicchio and arugula in a bowl. Toss with the remaining
   tablespoon of oil. Sprinkle with the vinegar and toss again. Divide
   the leaves among individual plates.

3 Preheat a ridged, cast-iron grill pan over high heat. Add the shrimp
   and grill for 2 minutes, turning and brushing with the marinade, until
   uniformly pink and cooked through. Arrange on top of the salad
   greens and sprinkle with the basil.

Second Trimester

Now you are in the fetal stage, which is the most rapid period of growth until birth, and you really begin to see your baby growing. The placenta now works to supply the fetus with nutrients and oxygen, leaving you less tired and nauseous, but your heartbeat and blood volume are both raised, making it important that you keep up your supplies of iron, magnesium, and vitamin B12. You need to provide quality nutrition to support your body and your baby's rapid growth and development.

As the hormone progesterone keeps rising to maintain your pregnancy, it may cause symptoms, such as constipation and heartburn. Increased blood flow can lead to nosebleeds, easy bruising, hemorrhoids, and varicose veins. Nutrition can help to prevent these or lessen their severity by encouraging good digestive and circulatory function.

(G) Growth of baby

(B) Brain development of baby

(A) Immunity-supporting antioxidants

(N) Natural remedy

(V) Suitable for vegetarians

(Q) Quick and easy to prepare

41

CAMOMILE

The mild sedatory effect of camomile tea can be a welcome relief at this stage, when thoughts about the developing pregnancy may interfere with sleep.

A growing belly can start to cause pelvic and back pain, and this together with breast tenderness makes some sleep positions uncomfortable. The chemicals apigenin and glycine in camomile soothe the body, making it easier to cope with discomfort and achieve a better quality of sleep. Camomile also has a refreshing effect, which has been known to help alleviate any nausea that may continue into the second trimester. Heartburn and constipation may be relieved by camomile because it helps to calm the nervous system, thus decreasing the stress that can contribute to these symptoms. The hippuric acid in camomile may also help prevent urinary tract infections (UTIs), which can result from the increasing pressure on the bladder and kidneys.

- Contains soothing apigenin and glycine, which help alleviate sleep problems.
- Camomile is a natural laxative and may ease digestive upsets.
- Hippuric acid helps keep UTIs, such as cystitis, at bay, which become more of a risk as blood flow increases.

Practical tips:
Don't drink herbal teas in large quantities during pregnancy because the effects of higher doses on the uterine muscle are still unclear. Place cold, used camomile tea bags on the eyes to relieve puffiness caused by insomnia or fluid retention. Avoid camomile if you are allergic to ragweed.

DID YOU KNOW?

Camomile tea is a popular sleep aid during pregnancy, but you only need one or two cups. Any more can have an opposite, stimulating effect, which is increased if you add sugar.

MAJOR NUTRIENTS PER 225 ml/ABOUT 1 CUP CAMOMILE TEA

Calories—approx*	2
Total fat	0 g
Protein	0 g
Fiber	0 g
Carbohydrate	0.47 g

* can vary greatly between varieties and strength of brew

Camomile infusion

SERVES 2 (N)(V)(Q)

*2 tbsp camomile flowers or two
    camomile tea bags*
⅓ cup sliced fresh ginger
2½ cups freshly boiled water
1–2 tsp honey (optional)
*ice cubes and lemon slices,
    to serve (optional)*

Method

1 If making the infusion in a teapot*, warm the pot first, then add
   the camomile flowers or bags and the ginger. Let the boiled water
   cool for a minute, then pour it into the teapot. Stir and let brew for
   3–5 minutes.

2 Strain and pour the infusion into two cups, adding honey to taste,
   if using. The tea can also be served as a refreshing cold drink with
   ice cubes and a slice of lemon.

* Alternatively, place 1 tablespoon of camomile flowers, or 1 bag,
   directly into each cup. Divide the ginger between the cups, then
   pour over the boiling water. Let the infusion steep for 5 minutes,
   then strain, if preferred. Add honey, if using.

42

BEEF

Eating beef occasionally will ensure the body is well equipped to regulate increasing hormone levels because it is high in the B vitamins and minerals.

During pregnancy, the body needs to make extra red blood cells, and the iron and vitamin B12 in beef enable this process. Meanwhile, the coenzyme Q-10 in beef helps create the necessary energy and supports the baby's heartbeat. Its B-vitamin profile facilitates protein metabolism, so that the mother can access the quality protein provided by the meat and use all these essential amino acids to build the baby's body. The zinc and selenium in beef also help the baby's tissues to grow, and keep the mother's own skin clear at a time when acne may be a problem due to increasing estrogen levels.

- The B vitamins and minerals regulate hormones, provide energy, and support both mother and baby physically and mentally.
- Contains iron and vitamin B12 to support the increasing need for new red blood cells.
- Coenzyme Q-10 generates energy in the cells, especially the growing fetal heart.
- A source of quality protein, made accessible by the B vitamins that are also in the meat, promoting baby's growth and development.
- Zinc and selenium help keep the complexion clear.

Practical tips:
You don't need to eat beef often to enjoy the benefits, so buy good, lean cuts, preferably from grass-fed, organic sources. Nonorganic meats contain potentially harmful hormones and antibiotics.

DID YOU KNOW?

As the need for energy increases, a dense protein, such as beef, can stop cravings for sugar. Instant energy sources in the form of cakes and cookies may be tempting, but they offer a baby little nutritional value.

MAJOR NUTRIENTS PER 100 G/3½ OZ GROUND BEEF

Calories	215
Total fat	15 g
Saturated fat	5.87 g
Monounsaturated fat	6.56 g
Protein	18.59 g
Carbohydrate	0 g
Fiber	0 g
Vitamin B3	4.65 mg
Vitamin B5	0.55 mg
Vitamin B6	0.35 mg
Vitamin B12	2.17 mcg
Iron	2.09 mg
Zinc	4.48 mg
Selenium	15.8 mcg

Sizzling lemongrass beef with asparagus

SERVES 4 (G)(B)(Q)

15 asparagus spears, trimmed
and diagonally sliced

2 tbsp vegetable oil

1 stalk lemongrass, peeled and
finely chopped

2½ cups bean sprouts

1 red bell pepper, thinly sliced

1 tbsp chopped garlic

1 lb tenderloin steak, thinly sliced

5 tbsp chicken stock

juice and finely sliced zest of 1 lime

pepper

Method

1 Bring a saucepan of water to a boil and quickly blanch the asparagus. Plunge into iced water.

2 Heat a wok over high heat and add the oil. Add the lemongrass, bean sprouts, red bell pepper, garlic, and beef and stir-fry for 1 minute. Add the stock, asparagus, and pepper to season, then stir-fry until the beef is done. Add the lime juice and zest, stir for another minute, and remove from the heat. Serve immediately.

43 DRIED FIGS

Dried figs provide a healthy energy source and have a better mineral profile than most other fruit and vegetables, closely resembling that of human breast milk.

As the pregnant body expands, it is important to keep up potassium levels in order to maintain the right mineral balance across the body's increasing fluids. This is especially true if sickness in the first trimester led to vomiting, because this depletes potassium and the other electrolyte minerals calcium, magnesium, and sodium, which work together for good nerve and muscle function. A diet high in vegetables and other whole foods should regulate the body's supplies naturally, but a deficiency in potassium is occasionally a problem. Electrolyte minerals, which are also contained in figs, should be kept up in pregnancy to prevent blood pressure from rising and becoming a complication.

- Contain high levels of potassium and other electrolyte minerals, which control nerve and muscle function.
- Help prevent common second trimester symptoms, such as fatigue, muscle cramps, and constipation.
- Help prevent high blood pressure, which may result in preeclampsia later in pregnancy.

Practical tips:
As snacks, dried figs can help provide a steady source of slow-release sugar to regulate energy levels and curb sugar cravings. A few figs a day will keep you regular but don't eat in excess, because they are very sweet and may even cause potassium-depleting diarrhea if you overindulge.

DID YOU KNOW?

Dried figs contain one of the highest fiber levels of any fruit and a protein-digesting latex called ficin. Snacking on them is a simple way to ward off pregnancy constipation.

MAJOR NUTRIENTS PER 25 G/ABOUT 3 DRIED FIGS

Calories	75
Total fat	0.28 g
Protein	0.99 g
Carbohydrate	19.16 g
Fiber	2.9 g
Calcium	49 mg
Magnesium	20 mg
Potassium	204 mg
Iron	0.61 mg

Baked stuffed honey figs

SERVES 4 (A)(N)(V)

⅔ cup fresh orange juice

6 tsp Greek honey

12 plumped dried figs

⅓ cup finely chopped, shelled
   pistachio nuts

3 tbsp very finely chopped,
   plumped dried apricots

1 tsp sesame seeds

Greek-style yogurt, to serve

Method

1 Preheat the oven to 350°F. Put the orange juice and 4 teaspoons
   of the honey in a saucepan and heat gently until the honey has
   dissolved. Add the figs and simmer for 10 minutes, or until softened.
   Remove from the heat and let the figs cool in the liquid.

2 Meanwhile, prepare the filling. Put the nuts, apricots, sesame seeds,
   and remaining 2 teaspoons of honey in a bowl and mix well.

3 Using a slotted spoon, remove the figs from the cooking liquid and
   reserve. Cut a slit at the top of each fig, where the stem joins.
   Using your fingers, plump up the figs and stuff each fig with about
   1 teaspoon of the filling mixture. Close the top of each fig and place
   in an ovenproof dish. Pour over the reserved cooking liquid.

4 Bake the figs in the preheated oven for 10 minutes, or until hot.
   Serve warm, or cold, with the sauce and Greek-style yogurt.

44 STRAWBERRIES

Strawberries contain many elements that aid circulation, supporting the needs of a growing baby in the second trimester, as it demands an increased supply of blood.

A baby's need for oxygen and nutrients, delivered via the blood, increases during this rapid stage of growth. This process must be supported by iron, necessary to make hemoglobin in blood, but often forgotten is vitamin C, which the body needs in order for iron to be absorbed. The vitamin C in strawberries also supports immunity, meaning a mother can ward off infection and be less likely to need medication and, together with the folate (folic acid) in this fruit, it is needed to make new cells for both mother and baby, and help prevent stretch marks. Along with the protective antioxidant proanthocyanidin in strawberries, vitamin C keeps the circulation flowing and blood vessels intact to help reduce common second trimester symptoms, such as nosebleeds, easy bruising, hemorrhoids, and varicose veins, all of which may result from higher blood volume.

- Vitamin C enables absorption of the iron needed to produce new red blood cells to nourish the baby.
- Contain vitamin C and folate to aid new growth for the fetus, and also help prevent or lessen stretch marks.
- Proanthocyanidin works with vitamin C to help prevent symptoms of poor circulation, such as nosebleeds and hemorrhoids.

Practical tips:

To boost antioxidant levels, add strawberries as a sweet treat to oatmeal, yogurt, or cereal. Remove the stem cap just before eating to preserve the high vitamin C content.

DID YOU KNOW?

The old wives' tale that eating strawberries during pregnancy causes strawberry marks has absolutely no basis in truth.

MAJOR NUTRIENTS PER 100 G/ABOUT 6 LARGE STRAWBERRIES

Calories	32
Total fat	0.3 g
Protein	0.67 g
Carbohydrate	7.68 g
Fiber	2 g
Vitamin C	58.8 mg
Potassium	153 mg
Folate	24 mcg
Lutein/Zeaxanthin	26 mcg

Breakfast berry smoothie

SERVES 1–2   (G) (A) (V) (Q)

8 oz strawberries, hulled
1 cup raspberries
⅔ cup milk
½ cup unsweetened muesli

Method

1 Reserve a strawberry for decoration, then place all the ingredients in a food processor or blender and process until almost smooth. Pour into glasses, top each smoothie with half a strawberry, and serve.

45

CHEDDAR CHEESE

Cheese can be a healthy addition to the diet during pregnancy when eaten with a lot of vegetables, omega-3 fatty acids, and very little refined sugar.

MAJOR NUTRIENTS PER 100 G/3½ OZ CHEDDAR CHEESE

Calories	403
Total fat	106 g
Saturated fat	21.09 g
Monounsaturated fat	9.39 g
Protein	24.9 g
Carbohydrate	1.28 g
Fiber	0 g
Vitamin B2	0.38 mg
Vitamin B5	0.41 mg
Vitamin B12	0.83 mcg
Vitamin A	1,002 IU
Vitamin D	12 IU
Choline	16.5 mg
Calcium	721 mg
Magnesium	28 mg
Potassium	98 mg
Iron	0.68 mg
Zinc	3.11 mg
Selenium	13.9 mcg

Cheese is high in saturated fat, the hard fat that has been so maligned in recent years. However, some intake of saturated fat is essential in order to enable cells to communicate with one another and to enhance our immunity against disease. Saturated fat is also needed to lend vital energy to the heart—it keeps the mother's pumping that extra blood around, while letting the baby's grow strong. Meanwhile, the calcium in cheese helps regulate the heartbeat, and the phosphorus and vitamin A also present let the calcium be moved easily into bone. The amino acid tryptophan in cheese enables us to make the "happy" brain chemical serotonin, and zinc is also crucial for a positive outlook. Quality protein and the B vitamins help to prevent the depression and moodiness that can sometimes accompany pregnancy.

• Saturated fat within a healthy diet supports nerve function, immunity, and heart health for both mother and baby.
• Phosphorus and vitamin A all help to lock essential calcium into new bone growth.
• Tryptophan, the B vitamins, and protein are important mood foods that help prevent pregnancy blues and moodiness.

Practical tips:
For taste and health, choose sharp cheddar cheese and eat in small amounts. When aged, the bacterial process cultivates fermenting bacteria and this can help your digestion.

Broccoli and cheese soup

SERVES 6 (G)(A)(V)(Q)

2 tbsp butter

1 onion, chopped

2 tsp chopped fresh tarragon,
   plus extra to garnish

3 cups peeled and grated potatoes

7 cups vegetable stock

1 broccoli, cut into small florets

1½ cups grated cheddar cheese

1 tbsp chopped fresh parsley

pepper

Method

1 Melt the butter in a large, heavy-bottom saucepan. Add the onion
   and cook, stirring occasionally, for 5 minutes, until softened. Add
   the tarragon with the potatoes, season with pepper to taste, and
   mix well. Pour in just enough of the stock to cover and bring to a
   boil. Reduce the heat, cover, and simmer for 10 minutes.

2 Meanwhile, bring the remaining stock to a boil in another saucepan.
   Add the broccoli and cook for 6–8 minutes, until just tender.

3 Remove both pans from the heat, let stand to cool slightly, then
   ladle the contents of both into a food processor or blender. Process
   until smooth, then pour the mixture into a clean saucepan. Stir
   the cheese into the pan with the parsley and heat gently to warm
   through, but do not let the soup boil. Ladle into warm soup bowls,
   garnish with tarragon, and serve immediately.

46 SCALLIONS

Scallions are rich sources of cleansing sulfur. Like all alliums (the onion family), including leeks and garlic, they help to keep toxins away from the baby as it grows.

The mineral sulfur has multiple detoxifying effects. It helps carry waste products out of both the mother's cells and the baby's, enabling nutrients to move in. It also promotes liver detoxification, thereby sweeping out toxic metals from the body. Sulfur, alongside the vitamin C and vitamin A present, is also needed to produce the collagen needed for skin and organs to be able to grow. Scallions contain much more vitamin K than normal white onions, and this is needed along with the phosphorus content to allow for calcium to form new bone. Eating onions may also prevent colds, a particular advantage at this stage, when the mucous membranes may be prone to swelling, causing nasal congestion and hampering the body's attempts to recover from infection.

- Cleansing sulfur removes toxins from cells via the liver, and facilitates an improved uptake of nutrients.
- Sulfur and vitamins C and A help generate collagen for new growth.
- Vitamin K and phosphorus aid mineralization of calcium into bone.
- Onions help prevent coughs and colds, which can be harder to overcome during pregnancy.

Practical tips:
All of the scallion can be eaten. Chopped finely and added to stir-fries, salads, or as a garnish for soups and stews, they provide refreshing crunch and bite. Choose bunches with clean white bulbs and leaves that look alive and healthy.

DID YOU KNOW?

Some women crave onions during pregnancy, while others cannot stand the smell or suddenly discover that they cause digestive upsets or indigestion. The milder scallion may be more tolerated than other varieties.

MAJOR NUTRIENTS PER 15 G/1 TBSP CHOPPED SCALLIONS

Calories	5
Total fat	0.03 g
Protein	0.27 g
Carbohydrate	1.10 g
Fiber	0.4 g
Vitamin C	2.8 mg
Vitamin A	150 IU
Vitamin K	31.1 mcg
Potassium	41 mg
Lutein/Zeaxanthin	171 mcg

Tomato and scallion twister

SERVES 1–2 Ⓖ Ⓐ Ⓝ Ⓥ Ⓠ

3 tomatoes
2 scallions, trimmed
1 cup fresh basil
1 garlic clove
ice cubes
shredded scallions, to garnish

Method

1 Place one tomato in a food processor or blender and firmly pack in the scallions, basil, and garlic, then top with the remaining tomatoes. Process all the ingredients, then pour into glasses with ice cubes. Top with shredded scallions and serve.

47

SESAME SEEDS

Sesame seeds are bundles of nutritional goodness. They make it easy to add essential fatty acids, antioxidants, and minerals to any meal.

The rich essential fatty acids sesame seeds contain support collagen production, promoting healthy all-round growth, and the fat-soluble nutrients vitamins A and E protect these fatty acids and the baby's eyes, brain, heart, and skin from damage. Sesamin and sesamolin, substances only found in sesame seeds, actually revitalize the vitamin E so that it can be used over again, while zinc transports vitamin A around the body and ensures the baby's lungs develop properly. Boasting the highest phytosterol content of any food, sesame seeds help keep the immune system regulated and reduce the risk of allergic reactions and sensitivities.

- Essential fatty acids, vitamin A, and vitamin E protect and support the growth of fatty areas in the baby's body.
- Sesamin and sesamolin revitalize vitamin E.
- Zinc takes vitamin A to where it is needed and supports lung development.
- Contain phytosterols that help prevent harmful inflammation.

Practical tips:
Choose the unhulled seeds, if possible, in order to benefit from the fiber, oils, fat-soluble vitamins, and minerals in the hull. Never cook with sesame seeds because the delicate essential fatty acids are easily damaged by heat. Sprinkle over stir-fries just before serving, and over salads and steamed vegetables. Tahini (sesame paste) has the added benefits of garlic and olive oil.

DID YOU KNOW?

Any information you may have heard about sesame seeds leading to miscarriage is erroneous and based on old wives' tales about "heating the body."

MAJOR NUTRIENTS PER 15 G/ABOUT 1½ TBSP SESAME SEEDS

Calories	86
Total fat	7.45 g
Monounsaturated fat	2.81 g
Omega-3 fatty acids	56.4 mg
Omega-6 fatty acids	3,205.8 mg
Protein	2.66 g
Carbohydrate	3.52 g
Fiber	1.8 g
Vitamin B3	0.68 mg
Vitamin B6	0.12 mg
Calcium	146 mg
Magnesium	53 mg
Iron	2.18 mg
Zinc	1.16 mg
Selenium	5.2 mcg

Golden tofu noodles with sesame seeds

SERVES 2 (G) (A) (V)

2 tsp virgin coconut oil

5 tbsp tamari

1 tbsp honey

*2-inch piece fresh ginger, peeled
and finely chopped*

*10½ oz firm tofu, drained, patted
dry, and cut into ½-inch slices*

6 oz soba noodles

1 tsp sesame oil

1 carrot, diced

3 radishes, sliced into rounds

2 scallions, diagonally sliced

½ cup diagonally halved snow peas

*small handful fresh cilantro leaves,
chopped*

1 tsp sesame seeds

pepper

Method

1 Preheat the oven to 375°F. Heat the coconut oil, 3 tablespoons of the
tamari, the honey, and half of the ginger in a wide saucepan, stirring
until combined. Remove from the heat, add the tofu, spoon the tamari
mixture over until coated, then set aside for 10 minutes.

2 Arrange the tofu on a nonstick baking sheet and roast for
20–25 minutes, turning once, until golden.

3 Meanwhile, cook the noodles in gently boiling water for 5 minutes,
or according to package directions, until tender. Drain, refresh under
cold running water until cool, then transfer to a bowl. Mix together
the remaining tamari, ginger, and sesame oil. Season with pepper
and pour over the noodles.

4 Add the carrot, radishes, scallions, snow peas, and cilantro to the
noodles. Turn the noodles gently until everything is combined.

5 To serve, divide the noodles between two plates, then scatter over
the sesame seeds and top with the tofu.

48

BEET

Beet works hard to support growth during pregnancy, while helping reduce the risk of damage to the fetus by protecting DNA and removing toxins.

As one of the richest food sources of folate (folic acid), beet encourages the all-round growth of the baby, while betacyanin, the antioxidant pigment that provides the rich color, helps protect DNA to minimize the risk of defects. Betaine, also present in beet, stimulates the liver cells to remove toxins that can interfere with development, and which may cause nausea, fatigue, and headaches. Beet contains a healthy dose of the mineral potassium which helps keep blood pressure and fluid balance regulated. The trace mineral silica allows calcium to be effectively incorporated into new bone growth.

DID YOU KNOW?

In the 16th century, beet was given as a "blood builder" to people who looked pale. Today we would say its high iron content was being used to treat anemia. It can be eaten during pregnancy to keep iron stores up.

- One of the best folate food sources to promote all growth.
- Betacyanin and betaine help protect DNA from damage to minimize the risk of growth defects.
- Betaine supports detoxification to help prevent headaches, tiredness, and nausea.
- Potassium helps regulate blood pressure and may help prevent water retention.
- Silica works with other bone nutrients to promote skeletal health in mother and baby.

MAJOR NUTRIENTS PER 100 G/3½ OZ BEET

Calories	43
Total fat	0.17 g
Protein	1.61 g
Carbohydrate	9.56 g
Fiber	2.8 g
Vitamin B3	0.33 mg
Vitamin B5	0.16 mg
Folate	109 mcg
Calcium	16 mg
Magnesium	23 mg
Potassium	325 mg
Iron	0.8 mg
Selenium	0.7 mcg
Betaine	128.7 mg

Practical tips:

Look for products without added vinegar if you tend to get yeast infections. The fresh root can be steamed or boiled, or roasted in a little olive oil, and is delicious eaten hot or cold.

Red cabbage and beet slaw

SERVES 4

4 cups finely shredded red
  cabbage
1 cup cooked, thin beet
  matchsticks
1 apple, cored and thinly sliced
1 tbsp lemon juice
1 tbsp sunflower seeds
1 tbsp pumpkin seeds
salt and pepper

Dressing
5 tbsp Greek-style yogurt
1 tbsp red wine vinegar
pepper

Method

1 Place the cabbage, beet, and apple slices in a large bowl. Add the lemon juice and mix well.

2 To make the dressing, place the yogurt and red wine vinegar in a bowl and mix together until smooth. Pour over the salad and stir well. Season with pepper, cover, and chill in the refrigerator for at least 1 hour.

3 Stir the salad thoroughly and adjust the seasoning to taste. Sprinkle with the sunflower and pumpkin seeds just before serving.

49 CHICKPEAS

Chickpeas (garbanzo beans) contain protein, complex carbohydrates, fiber, the B vitamins, and minerals, supporting aspects of growth, energy, immunity, and detoxification.

MAJOR NUTRIENTS PER 100 G/ABOUT ½ CUP CHICKPEAS, UNCOOKED

Calories	364
Total fat	6.04 g
Protein	19.3 g
Carbohydrate	60.65 g
Vitamin B3	1.54 mg
Vitamin B5	1.59 mg
Folate	557 mcg
Choline	95.2 mg
Calcium	105 mg
Magnesium	115 mg
Potassium	875 mg
Iron	6.24 mg
Selenium	13.9 mcg
Zinc	0.49 mg
Manganese	2.2 mg

Chickpeas and other legumes and beans are an important way to boost increased pregnancy protein needs for your baby's growth. Achieving these through plant as well as animal sources, such as meat, fish, and eggs, helps to maintain the correct, slightly alkaline balance in your body. This can ensure your body keeps good fluid balance and detoxification processes at a time of increased need. The slow-release complex carbohydrates and the B vitamins in chickpeas help to regulate energy and appetite to reduce the urge for quick-fix sugary foods that may exacerbate the energy dips and mood swings common in pregnancy. A good spread of minerals offers iron for red blood cell production, calcium, magnesium, and manganese for your baby's skeletal development, and selenium and zinc for antioxidant protection for you and your baby.

- Protein for optimal growth of your baby and in an alkaline form to help maintain fluid balance and detoxification.
- Carbohydrates, fiber, and the B vitamins ensure sustained energy levels to help reduce sugar cravings and energy and mood lows.
- Good mineral levels support growth and immune protection.

Practical tips:

Dried chickpeas can take a lot of soaking (between 12 and 24 hours) to prepare them for cooking, so these are easiest used from cans or jars. They are the main ingredient in hummus, easily prepared by blending with garlic, tahini, olive oil, and lemon juice.

Chickpea and potato soup

SERVES 4   (G) (B) (A) (V)

1 tbsp olive oil

1 large onion, finely chopped

2–3 garlic cloves, finely chopped
*   or crushed*

1 carrot, quartered and thinly sliced

2½ cups diced potatoes

¼ tsp garam masala

¼ tsp mild curry powder

14 oz of canned chopped
*   tomatoes (1¾ cups)*

3½ cups water

¼ tsp chili powder, or to taste
*   (optional)*

pinch of salt

14 oz of canned chickpeas
*   (garbanzo beans), drained and*
*   rinsed (1⅔ cups)*

½ cup fresh or frozen peas

pepper

chopped fresh cilantro, to garnish

Method

1 Heat the oil in a large saucepan over medium heat. Add the onion and garlic and cook, stirring occasionally, for 3–4 minutes, until the onion is beginning to soften. Add the carrot, potatoes, garam masala, and curry powder and continue cooking for another 1–2 minutes.

2 Add the tomatoes, water, and chili powder, if using, with the salt. Reduce the heat, cover, and simmer for 30 minutes, stirring occasionally.

3 Add the chickpeas and peas to the pan, then continue cooking for about 15 minutes, or until all the vegetables are tender. Taste the soup and adjust the seasoning, if necessary, adding a little more chili powder if you like. Ladle into warm soup bowls, sprinkle with chopped cilantro, and serve immediately.

50

TROUT

Trout supplies the healthy levels of fat needed to support a growing belly and also contribute to the fat developing under the baby's skin.

As an oily fish, the fats in trout are healthy omega-3 fatty acids. There are two kinds of omega-3 fatty acids: EPA, which supports heart and circulatory functions, and DHA, which is needed in high levels in the brain, central nervous system, and eyes. Some studies suggest that mothers with the highest levels of omega-3 fatty acids in their bodies have children who show better brain development up until the age of two, and even beyond, although the evidence is not conclusive. Our main source of vitamin D is sunlight, but food sources, such as trout, help keep up levels when light exposure is low, so that we receive vitamin D's positive effects on mood, bone health, and hormone levels. The B vitamins and omega-3 fatty acids also play vital roles in mood and energy regulation, helping to limit pregnancy blues and fatigue.

DID YOU KNOW?

The pink color of trout flesh comes from the fatty antioxidant astaxanthin, which is particularly neuroprotective. Eating trout will, therefore, help ensure the safety of the baby's brain and nervous system.

MAJOR NUTRIENTS PER 100 G/3½ OZ FRESH TROUT

Calories	148
Total fat	6.61 g
Omega-3 fatty acids—EPA	0.2 g
Omega-3 fatty acids—DHA	0.53 g
Protein	20.77 g
Carbohydrate	0 g
Fiber	0 g
Vitamin B1	0.35 mg
Vitamin B3	4.5 mg
Vitamin B5	1.94 mg
Vitamin B12	7.79 mcg
Vitamin D	155 IU

- Contains healthy oils that build up protective fat layers.
- Omega-3 fatty acids support heart, circulation, brain, eye, and motor functions in the developing baby.
- High levels of DHA in the diet may result in children with more advanced cognitive skills.
- Vitamin D, the B vitamins, and omega-3 fatty acids maintain mood and energy during pregnancy.

Practical tips:

Trout contains very low levels of mercury so is safe to eat during pregnancy, if within the 12 oz per week limit for fish and shellfish.

Marinated trout fillets

SERVES 4 (G) (B)

4 trout, cleaned and filleted
lemon wedges, to garnish
green beans and sautéed potatoes,
    to serve

Marinade

4 tsp vegetable oil
juice of ½ lemon
4 fresh fennel sprigs, finely
    chopped, plus extra to garnish
pepper

Method

1 To make the marinade, combine the oil and lemon juice in a small bowl and whisk together. Stir in the chopped fennel and a little pepper to taste.

2 Put the trout fillets in a shallow, nonmetallic dish. Pour over the fennel mixture, cover the dish with plastic wrap, and let marinate in the refrigerator for 30 minutes.

3 Remove the trout from the refrigerator and return to room temperature. Preheat a ridged grill pan over medium heat. Transfer the trout to the grill pan and brush the marinade over the fish. Cook the fillets for 5 minutes on each side, turning once and brushing with the remaining marinade.

4 Remove the trout from the grill pan and arrange on a serving dish. Garnish with fennel sprigs and lemon wedges, then serve immediately with green beans and sautéed potatoes.

51 PINTO BEANS

Pinto beans contain both protein and complex carbohydrates, regulating blood sugar levels, energy, and mood, and helping to prevent overeating during this trimester.

MAJOR NUTRIENTS PER 100 G/ABOUT ½ CUP DRIED PINTO BEANS

Calories	347
Total fat	1.23 g
Protein	21.42 g
Carbohydrate	62.55 g
Fiber	15.5 g
Vitamin B1	0.72 mg
Vitamin B2	0.21 mg
Vitamin B3	1.17 mg
Vitamin B5	0.79 mg
Vitamin B6	0.47 mg
Folate	525 mcg
Choline	66.2 mg
Calcium	113 mg
Magnesium	176 mg
Potassium	1,393 mg
Zinc	2.28 mg
Selenium	27.9 mcg

Pinto beans have a healthy all-round B-vitamin profile, enabling them to unlock their energy potential, and good levels of the lesser-known B-vitamin choline, in particular, which helps move fats through the liver and prevent nausea and bloating. Also included in the B vitamins is folate (folic acid), necessary for growth and red blood cell production throughout pregnancy. Lower levels of folic acid in the second trimester have been shown to increase the risk of preeclampsia in the third, and are generally associated with lower birth weights. The calcium, magnesium, and potassium in pinto beans are electrolyte minerals that support heart, brain, and muscle function in both mother and baby.

• Protein, slow-release carbohydrates, and the B vitamins regulate pregnancy energy and mood fluctuations.
• Choline helps reduce sickness and fluid retention.
• Folate supports fetal growth and lowers the risk of preeclampsia and low birth weight.
• Calcium, magnesium, and potassium regulate heart, muscle, and brain function.

Practical tips:
As with any bean, they can be used to make soups and stews and to add to salads. They also make great dips. Blend with olive oil, garlic, and lemon or even grapefruit juice. Serve with vegetable sticks or crackers as a convenient snack.

Vegetarian paella

SERVES 4–6 (G) (B) (A) (V)

½ tsp saffron strands

2 tbsp hot water

6 tbsp olive oil

1 onion, sliced

3 garlic cloves, crushed

1 red bell pepper, seeded and
    sliced

1 orange bell pepper, seeded and
    sliced

1 large eggplant, cubed

1 cup medium-grain paella rice

2½ cups vegetable stock

2½ cups peeled and chopped
    tomatoes

1½ cups sliced button mushrooms

1 cup halved green beans

14 oz of canned pinto beans
    (1⅔ cups)

pepper

Method

1 Put the saffron strands and water in a small bowl and let them infuse
   for a few minutes.

2 Meanwhile, heat the oil in a paella pan or wide, shallow skillet and
   cook the onion over medium heat, stirring, for 2–3 minutes, or until
   softened. Add the garlic, bell peppers, and eggplant and cook,
   stirring frequently, for 5 minutes.

3 Add the rice and cook, stirring continuously, for 1 minute, or until
   glossy and coated. Pour in the stock and add the tomatoes, saffron
   and its soaking water, and pepper to taste. Bring to a boil, then
   reduce the heat and let simmer, shaking the skillet frequently and
   stirring occasionally, for 15 minutes.

4 Stir in the mushrooms, green beans, and the pinto beans with their
   can juices. Cook for another 10 minutes, then serve immediately.

52 PECANS

Nuts provide the best fat, fiber, and carbohydrate package of any food. Pecans are also high in antioxidants and the B vitamins, ensuring the health of the baby.

At this stage, the baby is developing insulating fat under the skin, and fats are needed to supply this, as well as to help develop the fetal organs. The omega-9 fatty acids (monounsaturated fat) in pecans protect the baby's heart, while the magnesium and potassium help it beat regularly. The trace mineral manganese and the omega-3 fatty acids in these nuts are involved in developing the baby's brain structure. Meanwhile, the protein provided, together with manganese, folate (folic acid), and zinc, allow for the baby's body, from its tendons and ligaments to fingers and toes, to develop and grow.

DID YOU KNOW?

Pecans not only regulate blood sugar but also provide magnesium, low levels of which can lead to unstoppable cravings for chocolate.

- Provides energy and antioxidant protection against cell damage.
- Quality fats create a healthy fatty layer beneath the baby's skin.
- Monounsaturated fats, magnesium, and potassium ensure heart health.
- Manganese and omega-3 fatty acids support the baby's brain chemistry and development.
- Protein, manganese, folate and zinc help the baby's body structures to mature correctly.

MAJOR NUTRIENTS PER 25 G/¼ cup PECANS

Calories	207
Total fat	21.6 g
Monounsaturated fat	12.2 g
Omega-3 fatty acids	295 mg
Omega-6 fatty acids	6,189 mg
Protein	2.7 g
Carbohydrate	4.15 g
Fiber	2.8 g
Vitamin B1	0.19 mg
Vitamin B3	0.35 mg
Vitamin B5	0.25 mg
Folate	55 mcg
Magnesium	36 mg
Potassium	123 mg
Iron	1.4 mg
Manganese	1.25 mg
Zinc	1.25 mg
Phytosterols	32 mg

Practical tips:
Snack on a handful of pecans to help prevent blood sugar lows that can lead to dizziness or fainting. Blend in the blender to make an alternative to peanut butter. Avoid roasted nuts or cooking with pecans, because the essential fatty acids can be damaged.

Pear, pecan, and watercress salad

SERVES 2

*1 pear, halved, cored, and thinly
    sliced*
1 tsp lemon juice
¼ bunch watercress
¼ cup pecan halves

Dressing

2 tbsp extra virgin olive oil
½ tsp honey
½ tsp wholegrain mustard
2 tsp lemon juice
salt and pepper

Method

1 Toss the pear slices in the lemon juice to prevent them from browning.
2 Place the watercress in a large, shallow serving bowl and top with
    the pear. Scatter over the pecans.
3 To make the dressing, mix together the oil, honey, mustard, and
    lemon juice. Season with salt and pepper, then drizzle the dressing
    over the salad before serving.

53

CUCUMBER

Cucumber makes a refreshing, cooling, and soothing food at a time when dehydration can quickly lead to tiredness, headaches, and fluid retention.

One of cucumber's main benefits is its high water content, which together with the potassium and magnesium make it instantly hydrating and an effective tool in the prevention of high blood pressure. The trace mineral silica in cucumber provides support to the body's skin structures and will ease the expansion of skin around the belly as it grows. The potassium, vitamin C, and caffeic acid in cucumber help prevent any excess fluid around the ankles, wrists, fingers, and eyes. Caffeic acid, which has no relation to caffeine, is an antioxidant that displays anti-inflammatory and immune-regulating properties. It is particularly useful as an antifungal, helping prevent yeast infections in pregnancy that can be passed later to the child via the birth canal or if breast-feeding.

- Contains water, potassium, and magnesium, all of which are hydrating and help regulate blood pressure.
- Silica supports the structure of skin as it grows and expands.
- Potassium, vitamin C, and caffeic acid may have a positive effect on pregnancy puffiness.
- Caffeic acid supports immunity, reduces inflammation, and helps prevent fungal infection.

Practical tips:
Use cucumber slices as an effective remedy for tired and puffy eyes. To alleviate fluid retention, make an easy drink by blending cucumber with water and mint.

DID YOU KNOW?

Cucumber, and other foods with anti-inflammatory properties, can help ease aches and pains in pregnancy, such as the twinges felt in the second trimester as the ribcage expands to accommodate the baby.

MAJOR NUTRIENTS PER 100 G/ABOUT ⅓ CUCUMBER, WITH PEEL

Calories	16
Total fat	0.11 g
Protein	0.65 g
Carbohydrate	3.63 g
Fiber	0.5 g
Vitamin C	2.8 mg
Vitamin B5	0.26 mg
Magnesium	13 mg
Potassium	147 mg

Cucumber and tomato soup

SERVES 6 (G) (A) (N) (V)

4 tomatoes, peeled and seeded

4-inch piece of cucumber, peeled and seeded

2 scallions, green part only, chopped

3 lb 8 oz watermelon, rind removed and seeded

1 tbsp chopped fresh mint

salt and pepper

fresh mint sprigs, to garnish

Method

1 Put the tomatoes into a blender or food processor and, with the motor running, add the cucumber, scallions, watermelon, and mint. Season to taste with salt and pepper and process until smooth.

2 If you are not using a blender or food processor, push the watermelon through a strainer. Dice the tomatoes and add them to the melon mixture with the mint. Finely chop the cucumber and scallions and add to the mixture.

3 Chill the soup overnight in the refrigerator. Check the seasoning and transfer to a serving dish. Garnish with the mint sprigs and serve cold.

54 GRAPEFRUIT

Although grapefruit tastes very acidic, once processed in the body, it has a potent alkalizing effect that helps maintain the best possible environment for the baby.

Grapefruit helps our natural pH levels stay on track so that all processes can work efficiently. For the baby, this means a healthy exchange of nutrients and oxygen via the placenta. Vitamin C and bioflavonoids, including limonene, are antioxidants found in the white pith of grapefruit that help regulate the immune system and prevent sensitivities or intolerances being passed on to the baby. Along with selenium and the B vitamins in the fruit, these antioxidants help the liver process and expel toxins that may be harmful to a fetus. If you are on any medications, however, you should discuss grapefruit consumption with your doctor before including it in your diet because the substance naringin, found in the fruit, can affect the way medicines are metabolized.

- Alkalizing action counters the stressful effects of life's demands, pollution, and the occasional less-than-healthy foodstuff.
- Vitamin C and bioflavonoids regulate immunity, enabling the mother to pass on the benefits to her child.
- Vitamin C, limonene, selenium, and the B vitamins help liver detoxification to keep harmful substances away from the baby.

Practical tips:
Grapefruit is a natural and refreshing convenience food. Halve or peel and eat like an orange. If you don't like too sour a taste, try the pink variety because it is sweeter.

DID YOU KNOW?

Sour foods such as grapefruit can stimulate the digestive processes to help break down and absorb any food eaten afterward. They are a helpful appetizer when an expanding belly makes digestion harder.

MAJOR NUTRIENTS PER MEDIUM-SIZE HALF GRAPEFRUIT

Calories	39
Total fat	0.12 g
Protein	0.81 g
Carbohydrate	9.92 g
Fiber	1.3 g
Vitamin C	39.3 mg
Vitamin B3	0.32 mg
Vitamin B5	0.33 mg
Vitamin A	39 IU mcg
Potassium	175 mg
Selenium	1.7 mcg

Chicken and grapefruit salad

SERVES 4 Ⓖ Ⓐ

2 skinless, boneless chicken
    breasts, about 6 oz each
1 bouquet garni
few black peppercorns
2 pink grapefruit
3 Boston lettuces, separated
    into leaves
1 head Belgian endive, separated
    into leaves
fresh chervil sprigs, to garnish

Dressing

1 tbsp light olive oil
3 tbsp Greek-style yogurt
1 tsp wholegrain mustard
1 tbsp chopped fresh chervil
pepper

Method

1 Place the chicken in a large saucepan and pour over enough water
  to cover. Add the bouquet garni and peppercorns and bring to
  a gentle simmer. Cover and simmer for 25–30 minutes, until just
  cooked through. Let the chicken cool in the liquid.

2 Using a serrated knife, cut away the peel and pith from the
  grapefruit. Holding the fruit over a bowl to catch any juice, segment
  the flesh. Reserve 2 tablespoons of the juice.

3 Toss the salad greens in a bowl with the grapefruit segments.

4 To make the dressing, place all the ingredients in a small bowl with
  the reserved grapefruit juice. Whisk together until the dressing is
  thoroughly blended.

5 Drain the poached chicken and pat dry with paper towels. Tear into
  bite-size strips or thinly slice. Arrange on top of the salad greens.
  Drizzle over the dressing and garnish with chervil sprigs.

55 PARSLEY

Parsley contains a potent cocktail of antioxidants that provide protection from free radical damage to every cell of both mother and baby's growing body.

Parsley contains a mixture of the powerful antioxidants vitamin C, quercetin, luteolin, and rutin. They prevent damage from the continual onslaught of free radical damage from pollution and chemicals. They are also antihistamines, naturally bringing down inflammation and helping to prevent associated effects in pregnancy, including preeclampsia, bloating, and acne. These antioxidants strengthen and tone blood vessels to support blood flow to the baby and help prevent the bruising, varicose veins, and hemorrhoids that can become a problem as your pregnancy goes on. Extra antioxidant protection of the baby's nervous system, heart, eyes, and skin comes in the form of the carotenoids beta-carotene, lutein, and zeaxanthin.

- Antioxidants vitamin C, quercetin, luteolin, and rutin prevent damage to all body tissues.
- These also bring down inflammation and support circulation to help prevent common pregnancy symptoms, such as acne and hemorrhoids.
- Beta-carotene, lutein, and zeaxanthin support the health of the baby's eyes, skin, heart, and brain.

Practical tips:
The fresh, chopped herb can be added to the end of most dishes for extra greenery and nutrients. It also freezes well. Try adding to smoothies and juices and substitute for basil in pesto.

DID YOU KNOW?

Supplements of parsley oil should be avoided in pregnancy because they can cause early contractions, but the culinary use of all commonly used fresh or dried herbs is highly beneficial.

MAJOR NUTRIENTS PER 15 G/ABOUT 15 SPRIGS PARSLEY

Calories	3
Total fat	0.01 g
Protein	0.5 g
Carbohydrate	1 g
Fiber	0.5 g
Vitamin C	20 mg
Folate	23 mcg
Calcium	21 mg
Magnesium	8 mg
Potassium	83 mg
Iron	0.9 mg
Beta-carotene	758 mcg
Lutein/Zeaxanthin	834 mcg

Baked fish with parsley sauce

SERVES 2   (G) (B) (A) (Q)

extra virgin olive oil, for oiling
2 thick, white fish fillets, such
  as line-caught cod, haddock,
  or pollack, about 6 oz
4 slices lemon
pepper
salad greens, to serve

Parsley sauce

large handful fresh flat-leaf parsley,
  leaves removed
1 large garlic clove
4 tbsp extra virgin olive oil
1 tsp dried oregano
½ tsp ground cumin
large pinch of dried chile flakes

Method

1 Preheat the oven to 400°F. Lightly oil 2 pieces of aluminum foil with olive oil. Place a fish fillet in the center of each piece of foil, season with pepper, and top with the lemon slices. Fold up the edges of the foil to seal, then place the bundles on a baking sheet. Bake for 15–20 minutes, depending on the thickness of the fillets, until cooked.

2 Meanwhile, to make the sauce, put the parsley, garlic, oil, oregano, cumin, and chile flakes in a food processor or blender and process until combined.

3 Remove the fish bundles from the oven, open, and discard the lemon slices. Top the fish with the parsley sauce and serve with salad greens.

56

GLOBE ARTICHOKES

Globe artichokes provide an excellent boost of the essential minerals necessary to keep circulation, fluid levels, and bone development on track.

The minerals needed for the baby's growth and the mother's continuing health are called essential because they have to be obtained through the diet. If the diet doesn't provide enough, the body will make the baby its priority and the mother will have deficiency symptoms. Artichokes provide a good balance of calcium and magnesium, a lack of which can affect a mother's bone and tooth health and show up in symptoms, such as muscle cramps, headaches, and insomnia. An inadequate intake of potassium, also present in artichoke, will similarly lead to fatigue and muscle weakness. Artichokes also contain a substance called cynarin, which acts both as a mild laxative and increases bile flow from the liver to aid digestion and detoxification. The bioflavonoid apigenin in artichoke helps relax blood vessels and keep blood pressure within safe levels.

- Calcium and magnesium protect mother and baby's bone health, while relieving muscle aches and anxiety symptoms.
- Potassium wards off pregnancy fatigue and weakened muscles.
- Cynarin is a natural digestive aid and detoxification agent.
- Apigenin is a natural relaxant that eases blood vessels, preventing blood pressure from rising.

Practical tips:

Cook the fresh globes or, for convenience, add roasted artichoke hearts from deli counters to salads. Rub fresh artichoke with lemon juice as soon as it is prepared to avoid discoloration.

DID YOU KNOW?

Artichoke supplements are not advised during pregnancy because the concentrated extract detoxifies the body too intensely. However, it is perfectly safe to include artichokes naturally in the diet at this time.

MAJOR NUTRIENTS PER MEDIUM-SIZE GLOBE ARTICHOKE

Calories	60
Total fat	0 g
Protein	4.2 g
Carbohydrate	13.4 g
Fiber	6.5 g
Vitamin C	12 mg
Folate	65 mcg
Calcium	54 mg
Magnesium	72 mg
Potassium	425 mg
Iron	1.5 mg
Lutein/Zeaxanthin	557 mcg

Artichoke and arugula salad

SERVES 4   (G) (A) (V) (Q)

8 baby globe artichokes
juice of 2 lemons
bunch of arugula
3–4 tbsp extra virgin olive oil
4 oz Pecorino Romano cheese
pepper

Method

1 Break off the stem of each artichoke and trim about 1 inch off the top, depending on how young and small they are. Remove and discard any coarse outer leaves, leaving only the pale, tender inner leaves. Using a teaspoon, scoop out the chokes. Rub each artichoke with lemon juice as soon as it is prepared to prevent discoloration.

2 Thinly slice the artichokes and place in a salad bowl. Add the arugula, remaining lemon juice, and the oil, season with a little pepper to taste, and toss well.

3 Using a swivel-blade vegetable peeler, thinly shave the Pecorino Romano cheese over the salad, then serve immediately.

57 CARROT

The carotenoids that give carrots their vibrant color provide protection to the baby's fatty areas, including the brain, liver, skin, and eyes.

Although beta-carotene is the best known of the carotenoids, the alpha-carotene in carrots also stimulates protective antioxidant action within all fatty areas of the body. All cell walls, organs, and tissues incorporate fats, and these are continually open to damage. These carotenoids can also be stored in the liver and converted into vitamin A as we need it. Obtaining vitamin A from carrots during pregnancy is risk-free, because carotenes are not toxic if taken in excess, whereas high levels of preformed vitamin A are known to cause genetic mutations. Vitamin A is necessary in the right amount for cellular development, fighting infection, and to keep the placenta attached. Vitamin A deficiency in underdeveloped countries has been shown to result in maternal eye problems, lowered immune response, and anemia.

- Beta- and alpha-carotene prevent damage to the fats incorporated in all mother and baby's cells.
- Carotenes can be converted to vitamin A, vital for cell growth, placenta health, and immunity.
- A safe way of ingesting and storing vitamin A.

Practical tips:
Carrots are delicious raw, especially grated in salads, and will then release their starchy sugars more slowly. The fat-soluble carotenoids in carrots need oil present at the time of eating to carry the carotenoids from the digestive tract into the bloodstream.

DID YOU KNOW?

The carotenoids in carrots are particularly renowned for their heart protective effects—a bonus in pregnancy when your heart has to work much harder to pump blood to your baby and its volume increases.

MAJOR NUTRIENTS PER 100 G/ABOUT 2 SMALL CARROTS

Calories	41
Total fat	0.24 g
Protein	0.93 g
Carbohydrate	9.58 g
Fiber	2.8 g
Vitamin C	5.9 mg
Vitamin A	16,706 IU
Potassium	320 mg
Beta-carotene	8,285 mcg
Alpha-carotene	3,477 mcg

Creamy carrot and parsnip soup

SERVES 4 (**B**) (**A**) (**V**)

4 tbsp butter
1 large onion, chopped
8 carrots, chopped
2 large parsnips, chopped
1 tbsp peeled and grated fresh
*   ginger*
1 tsp grated orange rind
2½ cups vegetable stock
½ cup Greek-style yogurt
pepper
fresh cilantro sprigs, to garnish

Method

1 Melt the butter in a large saucepan over low heat. Add the onion and cook, stirring, for 3 minutes, until slightly softened. Add the carrots and parsnips, cover, and cook, stirring occasionally, for about 15 minutes, until the vegetables have softened a little.

2 Stir in the ginger, orange rind, and stock. Bring to a boil, then reduce the heat, cover, and simmer for 30–35 minutes, until the vegetables are tender. Remove from the heat and let cool for 10 minutes.

3 Transfer the soup to a food processor or blender and process until smooth. Return the soup to a clean pan, stir in the yogurt, and season well with pepper. Warm through gently over low heat.

4 Remove from the heat and ladle into warm soup bowls. Garnish each bowl with pepper and a sprig of cilantro, then serve.

58 BROWN RICE

Choosing to eat rice with its brown outer hull intact makes a fundamental difference to the health benefits that this food provides to both mother and baby.

The husk of brown rice is the part that contains the fiber, fats, minerals, and vitamins. The fiber is prebiotic, which means that it feeds your beneficial, probiotic digestive bacteria. This is a crucial consideration in pregnancy, because it ensures that the mother is producing anti-inflammatory antibodies on the walls of her intestines to prevent infection. The selenium and manganese in brown rice help to make antioxidant enzymes in the liver that both eliminate harmful elements in the body and also increase the action of antioxidants eaten in other food. Selenium can be converted into the coenzyme Q-10, needed alongside the B vitamins to create energy in all cells, especially in the hardworking hearts of mother and baby. The B vitamin choline is needed to make new cell walls, while the vitamin E in brown rice protects these from damage.

- Prebiotic fiber lowers a mother's risk of infection.
- Selenium and manganese make antioxidant enzymes that aid detoxification.
- Selenium makes coenzyme Q-10 to create energy in all cells, including both mother's and baby's hearts.
- Choline and vitamin E enable the creation of new cells.

Practical tips:

Choose long-grain instead of short-grain because it releases its sugars into the body more slowly. Brown basmati rice contains 20 percent more fiber than other varieties of brown rice.

DID YOU KNOW?

Brown rice can help curb sugar cravings during pregnancy because it is high on the "Satiety Index," which measures foods according to their ability to satisfy hunger. Brown rice will help you feel fuller for longer.

MAJOR NUTRIENTS PER 100 G/ABOUT ½ CUP BROWN RICE

Calories	370
Total fat	2.92 g
Omega-6 fatty acids	1,000 mg
Protein	7.94 g
Carbohydrate	77.24 g
Fiber	3.5 g
Vitamin B1	0.4 mg
Vitamin B3	5.09 mg
Vitamin B5	1.49 mg
Vitamin B6	0.51 mg
Choline	30.7 mg
Vitamin E	1.2 mg
Magnesium	143 mg
Iron	1.47 mg
Manganese	3.74 mg
Selenium	23.4 mcg
Zinc	2.02 mg

Vegetarian rice and lentils

SERVES 2 (G)(A)(V)

⅔ cup brown basmati rice, rinsed

1 tsp vegetable bouillon powder

3 cardamom pods, split

½ cup red split lentils

2 tbsp peanut oil

2 tbsp unsalted butter

1 onion, chopped

3 garlic cloves, chopped

1-inch piece fresh ginger, peeled
    and grated

1 tsp ground cumin

1 tsp ground coriander

1 tsp turmeric

½ tsp dried chile flakes (optional)

2 hard-cooked eggs, halved

2 tbsp chopped fresh cilantro,
    to garnish

pepper (optional)

Method

1 Put the rice in a saucepan and pour in enough water to cover by ½ inch. Bring to a boil, stir in the vegetable bouillon and cardamom, then reduce the heat to its lowest setting and cover with a tight-fitting lid. Let the rice simmer for 25 minutes, or until the water is absorbed and the grains are tender. Remove from the heat and let stand.

2 Meanwhile, put the lentils in a second pan, cover with water, and bring to a boil. Reduce the heat, partly cover, and simmer for 12–15 minutes, until tender. Drain well.

3 Heat the oil and butter in a large sauté pan and fry the onion for 6 minutes, until softened. Add the garlic, ginger, and spices and cook for another minute. Add the rice and lentils to the pan and stir until combined. Season with pepper, if not using the chile flakes.

4 Divide the rice mixture between two bowls and top each serving with a hard-cooked egg and fresh cilantro to garnish.

59

KALE

When we chew kale, or other cabbage family vegetables, such as broccoli, they release sulforaphanes, potent chemicals that boost the body's ability to remove toxins.

Vitamin E can help preserve the elasticity of a woman's skin as her belly and breasts expand. It is also known to support pregnancy generally; premature babies often show low vitamin E levels. Kale is an excellent source of vitamin K, which is involved in bone growth and needed to make thrombin, the substance that aids blood to clot. Kale supplies vitamin C, too, which is an important cofactor in the production of the estrogen and progesterone that maintain pregnancy. Very high levels of the carotenoids beta-carotene, lutein, and zeaxanthin in kale promote the optimal health of the baby's internal organs and eyes. They also protect the placenta from the toxins it holds back from the baby.

- Vitamin E helps prevent stretch marks and promotes a healthy full-term pregnancy.
- Vitamin K helps the baby's bones grow and reduces future risk of internal bleeding.
- Vitamin C is needed to produce the pregnancy hormones that sustain pregnancy.
- Contains sulforaphanes and carotenoids that protect the placenta and the baby from toxic damage.

Practical tips:
To retain the most goodness, steam or stir-fry instead of boil, and chop the leaves at the very last moment. Kale can also be made into crispy snacks by baking in pieces for 5–7 minutes.

DID YOU KNOW?

The indole-3-carbinole in cabbage family vegetables promotes DNA repair and may stop cancer-cell growth. This action can be transmitted from mother to baby and may help prevent cancers as they grow.

MAJOR NUTRIENTS PER 100 G/3½ OZ KALE

Calories	50
Total fat	0.7 g
Protein	3.3 g
Carbohydrate	10 g
Fiber	2 g
Vitamin C	120 mg
Vitamin E	1.7 mg
Vitamin K	817 mcg
Folate	29 mcg
Calcium	135 mg
Magnesium	34 mg
Potassium	447 mg
Iron	1.7 mg
Beta-carotene	9,226 mcg
Lutein/Zeaxanthin	39,550 mcg

Beans and greens stew

SERVES 4   (G) (A) (V)

*1½ cups dried cannellini beans,
    soaked overnight*

1 tbsp olive oil

2 onions, finely chopped

4 garlic cloves, finely chopped

1 celery stalk, thinly sliced

2 carrots, halved and thinly sliced

5 cups water

¼ tsp dried thyme

¼ tsp dried marjoram

1 bay leaf

4½ oz kale

pepper

Method

1 Drain the beans, put them in a saucepan, and add enough cold water to cover them by 2 inches. Bring to a boil and boil for 10 minutes. Drain and rinse well.

2 Heat the oil in a large saucepan over medium heat. Add the onions and cook, covered, for 3–4 minutes, stirring occasionally, until the onions are just softened. Add the garlic, celery, and carrots, and continue to cook for another 2 minutes.

3 Add the water, drained beans, thyme, marjoram, and bay leaf and bring to a boil. When the mixture begins to bubble, reduce the heat to low. Cover and simmer gently, stirring occasionally, for about 1¼ hours, until the beans are tender. Season with pepper.

4 Let the soup cool slightly, then transfer 2 cups to a food processor or blender. Process until smooth, then return to the stew.

5 Slice the kale widthwise into thin ribbons, keeping the tender leaves separate. Add the thicker leaves and cook gently, uncovered, for 10 minutes. Stir in any remaining kale and continue cooking for 5–10 minutes, until all the greens are tender.

6 Taste and adjust the seasoning, if necessary. Ladle into warm soup bowls and serve.

60 GREEN BEANS

All beans contain protein, complex carbohydrates, and soluble fiber, but green beans are the seed pods themselves, and, therefore, contain cleansing insoluble fiber.

In pregnancy, removing toxins from the body before they can do harm becomes even more imperative, because the placenta may not be able to filter out everything that the body is exposed to. Insoluble fiber is particularly good at absorbing toxic matter and excess salts. At the same time, it draws water into stools, regulating digestion and easing any problems with constipation or diarrhea. The vitamin C and B vitamins in green beans also support the health of the intestines. Choose green beans to balance the blood sugar and provide slow-release energy. All foods that do this help to regulate weight and appetite, thereby encouraging an expectant mother to put on weight steadily and appropriately by making the right food choices.

- Insoluble fiber removes toxins that may harm the fetus, and regulates bowel function to prevent constipation or diarrhea.
- Fiber, vitamin C, and the B vitamins support digestive health.
- Green beans regulate energy and appetite, encouraging only appropriate weight gain.

Practical tips:
Green beans, along with string beans and snow peas are seed pods with tiny seed forms of the bean inside and can be eaten whole. Steam, boil, or add to soups, stews, or stir-fries. Green beans are an easy way to add some protein to a simple vegetable dish.

DID YOU KNOW?
Green beans provide a healthy dose of fiber, keeping the body regular when the bowel muscle relaxes and sometimes slows down. The relaxing of muscles is due to the pregnancy hormone relaxin, which allows the womb to stretch.

MAJOR NUTRIENTS PER 100 G/ABOUT 1 CUP GREEN BEANS

Calories	31
Total fat	0.1 g
Protein	1.8 g
Carbohydrate	7.1 g
Fiber	3.6 g
Vitamin C	16 mg
Vitamin B2	0.1 mg
Vitamin B3	0.7 mg
Vitamin B5	0.2 mg
Vitamin B6	0.1 mg
Folate	33 mcg
Choline	15.3 mg

Green bean and potato curry

SERVES 2–4 Ⓖ Ⓐ Ⓥ Ⓠ

3 tbsp vegetable oil

1 tsp white cumin seeds

1 tsp mixed mustard and onion
seeds

3 fresh tomatoes, sliced

1 tsp finely chopped fresh ginger

1 tsp crushed fresh garlic

1 tsp chili powder

2 cups diagonally sliced, 1-inch
green beans pieces

2 potatoes, peeled and diced

1¼ cups water

chopped fresh cilantro, to garnish

Method

1 Heat the oil in a large, heavy-bottom saucepan. Add the white
cumin seeds and the mustard and onion seeds, stirring well.

2 Add the tomatoes to the pan and stir-fry the mixture for
3–5 minutes.

3 Mix together the ginger, garlic, and chili powder in a bowl and add
to the pan. Stir until combined. Add the green beans and potatoes
to the saucepan and stir-fry for 5 minutes.

4 Add the water to the saucepan, reduce the heat, and simmer for
10–15 minutes, stirring occasionally. Transfer to a warm serving
dish, garnish with chopped cilantro, and serve.

Third Trimester

The last months of pregnancy are a period of intense growth. If you are not eating healthily, your own energy and health can be affected because your baby's requirements are so high. However, it is only during this trimester that you actually need more calories; just 10 percent more, so an extra snack or few slices of bread daily will be sufficient. Ensuring your extra food has high nutritional value is crucial, especially because less room in your stomach means you may need to eat little and often.

Protein needs are high to provide building blocks for your baby's growing body, and foods that supply this and the growth nutrients folate (folic acid), zinc, and vitamin C are key. Minerals, such as magnesium, calcium, and potassium support the bone health and heartbeat of both mother and baby.

(G) Growth of baby

(B) Brain development of baby

(A) Immunity-supporting antioxidants

(N) Natural remedy

(V) Suitable for vegetarians

(Q) Quick and easy to prepare

61 ADZUKI BEANS

Adzuki beans contain protein, fiber, and carbohydrates. They are also rich in many nutrients that sustain intense growth during this last trimester.

MAJOR NUTRIENTS PER 100 G/ABOUT ½ CUP ADZUKI BEANS

Calories	329
Total fat	0.53 g
Protein	19.87 g
Carbohydrate	62.9 g
Fiber	12.7 g
Vitamin B1	0.45 mg
Vitamin B2	0.22 mg
Vitamin B3	2.63 mg
Vitamin B5	1.47 mg
Vitamin B6	0.35 mg
Folate	622 mcg
Calcium	66 mg
Magnesium	127 mg
Potassium	1,254 mg
Phosphorus	381 mg
Iron	4.98 mg
Zinc	5.04 mg

One of these nutrients is zinc, low levels of which have been shown to result in lower birth weights. With less room available for the mother's stomach, zinc is also important in keeping up appetite, encouraging a little-but-often eating regime of nutrient-dense foods. The folate (folic acid) in adzuki beans is used to make the DNA that facilitates growth as well as the extra red blood cells needed at this stage of pregnancy, when blood volume has increased by 40–50 percent. The high magnesium and potassium levels in the beans assist this process by enabling the heart muscle to keep circulation flowing to the womb and reduce common third trimester symptoms, such as high blood pressure, puffiness, fatigue, and muscle cramps.

- Provide nutrients for growth, energy, and detoxification, including zinc, which enables the baby to grow to optimal size.
- Zinc also keeps appetite strong so that both mother and baby can keep up their energy levels.
- Folate supports DNA and red blood cell production for growth.
- Magnesium and potassium keep up the circulation and help prevent high blood pressure, bloating, and cramps.

Practical tips:
Adzuki beans can be bought precooked and frozen, and are ideal for slow cooking. Add them cooked to vegetable soups to bulk up the protein content.

Spicy adzuki bean stew

SERVES 2 (G) (A) (V)

3½ cups dried adzuki beans,
    soaked overnight
2 tbsp vegetable oil
1 large onion, chopped
3 garlic cloves, chopped
1 celery stalk, sliced
2 carrots, sliced
1½-inch piece fresh ginger, peeled
    and sliced into rounds
1 tsp ground cumin
2 tsp ground coriander
3 cardamom pods, split
1¼ cups vegetable stock
3½ cups baby spinach leaves
pepper

Method

1 Drain and rinse the soaked adzuki beans, then transfer to a pan, cover with plenty of water, and bring to a boil. Reduce the heat to low, cover the pan, and simmer the beans for 40–50 minutes, until tender, then drain.

2 Meanwhile, heat the oil in a pan and sauté the onion for 6 minutes, until softened. Add the garlic, celery, and carrots and cook, stirring, for another 5 minutes. Stir in the spices, add the stock, and simmer, partly covered, for 10 minutes. Set aside.

3 When the adzuki beans are tender, drain and transfer them to the pan with the onion mixture. Add the spinach and reheat for 5 minutes, or until wilted. Season with pepper, and remove the ginger and cardamom before serving.

62 CHERRIES

Cherries make a superior sweet treat. They taste delicious and, unlike cakes and cookies, bring balance to your blood sugar instead of robbing you of energy.

At this stage, the baby is producing around 100,000 new brain cells a minute, but these are easily damaged or destroyed by free radicals. Free radicals are unstable molecules that enter the body via pollution and chemicals, cooked foods, electrical equipment, and our natural metabolic processes. The proanthocyanidins in cherries, which are demonstrated by the deep red color of the fruit, are antioxidant bioflavonoids that quench free radicals. Working alongside the vitamin C in the fruit, they also have an anti-inflammatory action, helping prevent preeclampsia and skin problems and relieving pain. Antioxidants also support the mother's immunity, which is directly passed on to the baby, helping prevent illness that can take energy away from the vital process of growth.

- Antioxidants destroy harmful toxins to protect the growing baby's brain.
- Proanthocyanidins work with vitamin C to help prevent inflammation and infection in both mother and baby.

Practical tips:
For taste and to get the most vitamin C, cherries are best eaten fresh, with stems intact. Choose darker colors for more proanthocyanidin content. Think of them as a wonderful treat— both delicious and healthy, if also on the pricey side. A portion of cherries now and then will help keep your bowels regular when they may be sluggish.

DID YOU KNOW?

The antioxidants provided by cherries play a major role in curbing inflammation. They work most effectively when included in a diet high in omega-3 fatty acids, which can be obtained from oily fish, nuts, and seeds.

MAJOR NUTRIENTS PER 100 G/ABOUT ¾ CUP CHERRIES

Calories	63
Total fat	0 g
Protein	1.06 g
Carbohydrate	16.01 g
Fiber	2.1 g
Vitamin C	7 mg
Potassium	222 mg
Lutein/Zeaxanthin	85 mcg

Cherry sundae

SERVES 2

5½ oz strawberries, hulled
1–2 tsp honey, to taste
1 tsp vanilla bean paste or extract
1 cup plain yogurt with live cultures
1 cup fresh cherries, stoned and
*   halved*
⅓ cup coarsely chopped hazelnuts

Method

1 Put the strawberries in a food processor or blender and process until pureed. Transfer to a bowl, then stir in the honey and vanilla bean paste. Stir the strawberry and vanilla sauce into the yogurt.

2 Divide the cherries between 2 tall glasses, then top with the strawberry yogurt mixture. Scatter over the chopped hazelnuts before serving.

63 PINEAPPLE

At this stage of pregnancy, the mother may crave sugar to satisfy the baby's energy requirements. Pineapple is a healthy and nutritious way to deal with these cravings.

In the third trimester, the baby begins to squash the mother's digestive organs and reduce her stomach volume. As the belly grows, higher levels of the hormone relaxin, which relaxes the esophagus and reduces the efficiency of the digestive muscles, can cause constipation and heartburn. Pineapple helps all the digestive processes and relieves these symptoms. It also contains vitamin C and the mineral manganese, which safeguard the increased production of sex hormones needed to maintain the pregnancy and induce labor at the right time. These nutrients also support blood sugar balance, providing constant energy to both mother and baby. They are necessary, too, for bone development.

- Helps digestive actions, relieving constipation and heartburn.
- Vitamin C and manganese allow for the pregnancy sex hormones to rise appropriately and eventually induce labor. They also enable rapid bone development.
- Pineapple helps steady blood sugar balance, providing energy to all cells and for growth.

Practical tips:
In many cultures, pineapple is avoided until the very end of pregnancy because it is believed to soften the cervix and bring on labor. In fact, you would need to eat a huge amount to achieve this effect, which anyway remains unproven. A few slices is nothing to be concerned about, and helps digestion when eaten after a meal.

DID YOU KNOW?

Along with nipple stimulation, sex, and curry, eating a lot of pineapple is believed to help induce labor when overdue, because the stimulating action of the digestive system encourages contractions.

MAJOR NUTRIENTS PER MEDIUM-SIZE FRESH PINEAPPLE SLICE

Calories	40
Total fat	0 g
Protein	0.5 g
Carbohydrate	10.6 g
Fiber	1.2 g
Vitamin C	43 mg
Magnesium	41 mg
Potassium	97 mg
Manganese	148 mg

Sweet-and-sour fish salad

SERVES 4   (**G**)(**A**)(**N**)(**Q**)

8 oz trout fillets, rinsed
8 oz white fish fillets
(such as haddock or cod)
1¼ cups water
1 lemongrass stalk
2 lime leaves
1 large red chile
1 bunch scallions, trimmed
and shredded
⅔ cup diced fresh pineapple
1 small red bell pepper, seeded
and diced
1 bunch watercress, washed
and trimmed
snipped fresh chives, to garnish

Dressing
1 tbsp sunflower oil
1 tbsp rice wine vinegar
pinch of chili powder
1 tsp honey
pepper

Method

1 Place the fish in a skillet and pour over the water. Bend the lemongrass in half to bruise it and add to the skillet with the lime leaves. Prick the chile with a fork and add to the skillet. Bring to a boil, reduce the heat, and simmer for 7–8 minutes. Let cool.

2 Drain the fish thoroughly, flake the flesh away from the skin, and place in a bowl. Gently stir in the scallions, pineapple, and bell pepper.

3 Arrange the watercress on 4 serving plates and spoon the cooked fish mixture on top.

4 To make the dressing, mix together the first four ingredients and season with a little pepper. Spoon over the fish and serve garnished with snipped chives.

64 DRIED PLUMS

Dried plums (prunes) contain the natural laxative dihydrophenylisatin, which, together with their fiber content, helps keep a sluggish pregnancy bowel regular.

Dried plums offer a much safer and gentler alternative to laxatives, such as senna and cascara. Both the squashing of the digestive organs and colon, and the effect on the muscles of the pregnancy hormone relaxin, can cause a slowdown. This is not only uncomfortable, but can also cause a toxic buildup, while any straining and lower bowel pressure increases the risk of hemorrhoids. The antioxidants vitamin C and rutin in dried plums help prevent piles by keeping the veins intact, and, therefore, also help relieve any tendency to easy bruising and varicose veins. The fiber pectin soaks up toxic metals, such as mercury, aluminum, and lead, stopping them from reaching the baby. Meanwhile, the carotenoids beta-carotene, lutein, and zeaxanthin provide antioxidant protection for the baby's brain and eyes.

- Gentle laxative action removes toxins.
- Vitamin C and rutin help prevent hemorrhoids, as well as varicose veins and bruising.
- Fatty antioxidant carotenoids protect the growing baby's brain and eyes.

Practical tips:
Dried plums are extremely satisfying snacks that, although sweet, help regulate blood sugar levels. To relieve constipation, make a dried plum puree by combining with boiling water in a blender, and add to muesli or oats.

DID YOU KNOW?

Prunes and dried plums are the same thing. Their sugar content becomes concentrated during the drying process. They offer a quick energy source during late pregnancy.

MAJOR NUTRIENTS PER 100 G/ABOUT 11 DRIED PLUMS

Calories	240
Total fat	0.38 g
Protein	2.18 g
Carbohydrate	63.88 g
Fiber	7.1 g
Calcium	43 mg
Magnesium	41 mg
Beta-carotene	394 mcg
Lutein/Zeaxanthin	148 mcg

Spicy vegetable and dried plum stew

SERVES 4 (B) (A) (N) (V)

2 tbsp olive oil

1 onion, finely chopped

2–4 garlic cloves, crushed

1 red chile, seeded and sliced

*1 eggplant, about 8 oz, cut into
    small chunks*

*small piece fresh ginger, peeled
    and grated*

1 tsp ground cumin

1 tsp ground coriander

*pinch of saffron strands
    or ½ tsp turmeric*

1–2 cinnamon sticks

*½ butternut squash, peeled,
    seeded, and cut into
    small chunks*

*1 sweet potato, cut into
    small chunks*

1 cup plumped dried plums

2–2½ cups vegetable stock

4 tomatoes, chopped

*14 oz of canned chickpeas
    (garbanzo beans), drained
    and rinsed (1⅔ cups)*

*1 tbsp chopped fresh cilantro,
    to garnish*

Method

1 Heat the oil in a large, heavy-bottom saucepan with a tight-fitting
lid and cook the onion, garlic, chile, and eggplant, stirring frequently,
for 5–8 minutes, until softened. Add the ginger, cumin, coriander,
and saffron and cook, stirring continuously, for 2 minutes. Bruise
the cinnamon.

2 Add the cinnamon, squash, sweet potato, dried plums, stock,
and tomatoes to the saucepan and bring to a boil. Reduce the
heat, cover, and simmer, stirring occasionally, for 20 minutes. Add
the chickpeas to the saucepan and cook for another 10 minutes.
Discard the cinnamon and serve garnished with fresh cilantro.

65 TURKEY

Turkey combines the B vitamins and protein for a boost to energy and growth. It also helps to keep up mood, so that you can cope with stress and sleep well.

The vitamin B3 in turkey is particularly skilled at helping the body tissues to use oxygen. A mother's body will prioritize her baby's growth over her own, but it's vital to stay healthy to prepare for birth, postnatal recovery, and breast-feeding. Vitamin B6 levels are known to drop dramatically during pregnancy and this can result in skin problems and depression. Turkey contains good levels of all the mood-enhancing B vitamins, as well as the amino acid tryptophan, from which we make serotonin, the sleep and mood brain chemical that helps us stay relaxed and positive. The brown meat in turkey contains higher levels of the energizing nutrient coenzyme Q-10, which provides valuable energy and protection for the baby's heart muscle.

- Vitamin B3 oxygenates both mother's and baby's body tissues, promoting growth and repair.
- The B vitamins help maintain good skin and mood.
- Tryptophan makes serotonin to regulate mood and sleep.
- Contains coenzyme Q-10, which keeps energy firing in all cells, including the baby's heart.

Practical tips:
Cravings for sugar generally signify a need for more quality fat and protein in the diet. When experiencing fatigue, a few good-quality slices of turkey—organic, if possible—with cucumber or avocado on rye crackers can help.

....

DID YOU KNOW?

By now, protein requirements will have increased by up to one-third compared to pre-pregnancy. Turkey provides a high-quality source, containing all of the amino acids necessary for growth.

....

MAJOR NUTRIENTS PER 100 G/3½ OZ TURKEY, SKIN REMOVED

Calories	111
Total fat	0.65 g
Saturated fat	0.21 g
Monounsaturated fat	0.11 g
Protein	24.6 g
Carbohydrate	0 g
Fiber	0 g
Vitamin B3	6.23 mg
Vitamin B5	0.72 mg
Vitamin B6	0.58 mg
Iron	1.17 mg
Zinc	1.24 mg
Glutamic acid	4.02 g

Turkey and rice salad

SERVES 4 (G) (B) (A)

4 cups chicken stock

1 cup mixed long-grain and
wild rice

2 tbsp olive oil

8 oz skinless, boneless turkey
breast, cut into thin strips

3½ cups snow peas

4 oz oyster mushrooms, torn
into pieces

1 cup shelled pistachio nuts,
finely chopped

2 tbsp chopped fresh cilantro

1 tbsp snipped fresh garlic chives

1 tbsp balsamic vinegar

pepper

snipped fresh chives, to garnish

Method

1 Reserve 3 tablespoons of the stock and bring the remainder to
a boil in a large saucepan. Add the rice and cook for 30 minutes,
or until tender. Drain and let cool slightly.

2 Meanwhile, heat 1 tablespoon of the oil in a preheated wok or
skillet. Stir-fry the turkey over medium heat for 3–4 minutes, or until
cooked through. Using a slotted spoon, transfer the turkey to a
dish. Add the snow peas and mushrooms to the wok and stir-fry for
1 minute. Add the reserved stock, bring to a boil, then reduce the
heat, cover, and simmer for 3–4 minutes. Transfer the vegetables
to the dish and let cool slightly.

3 Thoroughly mix the rice, turkey, snow peas, mushrooms, nuts,
cilantro, and garlic chives together, then season to taste with
pepper. Drizzle with the remaining oil and the vinegar and garnish
with fresh chives. Serve warm.

66 LEEKS

Leeks have a well-deserved reputation as a gentle natural laxative and detoxifying agent, which makes them a perfect choice at a time when the bowel may be slow.

All members of the allium (onion) plant family—leeks, onions, and garlic—have a high sulfur content, which helps the liver detoxify harmful substances. This mineral also moves waste products out of individual cells, allowing for nutrients to enter. Leeks have high levels of prebiotic fibers, such as inulin, which feed the probiotic beneficial bacteria in your intestines and keep your bowels moving. These prebiotics help you fight infection and encourage good immune responses throughout the body, and convert the plant foods that you eat into energy. All of these actions are important in helping to keep harmful toxins away from the baby. The antibodies that a mother's immune system produces against fungal, viral, or bacterial invaders are passed to the fetus through the placenta.

- High sulfur content detoxifies the body and lets nutrients into cells that protect and nourish the baby.
- Prebiotic fiber inulin feeds good digestive bacteria to prevent constipation that can cause toxic buildup.
- Prebiotics also support immunity against invading bacteria and viruses, which is passed on to the baby.

Practical tips:
Leeks can be used in any recipe in place of onion, which may exacerbate heartburn tendencies in the third trimester. Be careful not to overcook leeks because they easily become soggy and lose their flavor. Use them as a base for a vegetable broth or soup.

DID YOU KNOW?
Leeks, along with onions, garlic, spinach, parsley, and carrots, contain the substance sulfoquinovosyl diacylglycerol, which is known to stop cancer cells from growing and may help prevent the risk of childhood cancers in the unborn baby.

MAJOR NUTRIENTS PER MEDIUM-SIZE LEEK

Calories	54
Total fat	0.27 g
Protein	1.33 g
Carbohydrate	12.59 g
Fiber	1.6 g
Vitamin C	10.7 mg
Vitamin B6	0.21 mg
Vitamin K	41.8 mcg
Folate	57 mcg
Calcium	53 mg
Magnesium	25 mg

Leek and herb soufflés

SERVES 4 (B) (A) (V)

1 tbsp olive oi
12 oz baby leeks, finely chopped
½ cup vegetable stock
½ cup walnuts
2 eggs, separated
2 tbsp chopped mixed herbs
2 tbsp plain yogurt with live cultures
butter, for greasing
pepper

Method

1 Preheat the oven to 350°F. Heat the oil in a skillet. Add the leeks and sauté over medium heat, stirring occasionally, for 2–3 minutes.

2 Add the stock to the leeks in the skillet, reduce the heat, and simmer gently for an additional 5 minutes.

3 Place the walnuts in a food processor or blender and process until finely chopped. Add the leek mixture to the nuts and process briefly to form a puree. Transfer to a mixing bowl.

4 Mix together the egg yolks, the herbs, and the yogurt until thoroughly combined. Pour the egg mixture into the leek puree. Season with pepper to taste and mix well.

5 In a separate, grease-free mixing bowl, whisk the egg whites until firm peaks form.

6 Fold the egg whites into the leek mixture. Spoon the mixture into four ⅔-cup ovenproof ramekins lightly greased with butter and place on a warm baking sheet.

7 Cook in the preheated oven for 35–40 minutes, or until well risen and set. Serve the soufflés immediately.

67

RASPBERRY LEAF TEA

Raspberry leaf tea, which is thought to ease birth pain and complication, has a long-standing tradition as a herbal support during the third trimester.

Raspberry leaf tea contains an alkaloid called fragine, which helps tone and strengthen the uterine and pelvic muscles. This effect may help shorten the second stage of labor. More effective muscle contractions can help reduce pain because the muscles remain oxygenated and don't build up lactic acid through stress. Some studies have shown that these effects may result in less intervention during labor: specifically, fewer Caesarean and forceps deliveries in those women who had regularly drunk it in their third trimester. In one study, two-thirds of midwives recommended raspberry leaf tea as a known remedy to help women. The tea's rich and varied mineral content is also believed to help birth.

- Fragine tones muscles in the womb and pelvis to make contractions stronger during labor.
- May help shorten the second stage of labor, reduce labor pains, and reduce the likelihood of intervention.
- Its rich mineral content, although not quantified, is believed to aid muscle contractions.

Practical tips:
Due to its effects on the uterus, many sources recommend waiting until week 36 of pregnancy before drinking raspberry leaf tea. If the pregnancy has had any serious complications, first consult your health-care provider. Drink 1–2 cups per day of the fresh leaf infusion or, if using tea bags, 2–3 cups.

DID YOU KNOW?
The alkaloids in raspberry leaf tea that prepare the uterus for labor may also help to shrink it back to normal size after birth, as well as encourage the production of breast milk.

MAJOR NUTRIENTS PER 225 ML/ABOUT 1 CUP RASPBERRY TEA

Calories—approx*	2
Total fat	0 g

* No other data available—it is not researched/quantified

Raspberry leaf punch

SERVES 2 (A)(N)(V)(Q)

1 raspberry leaf tea bag
1¼ cups just-boiled water
1 cup raspberry juice
½ cup orange juice
½ apple, cored and sliced into
    half moons
6 slices cucumber, halved
few fresh mint leaves
ice cubes, to serve (optional)

Method

1 Prepare a cup of raspberry leaf tea using the water. Let cool and remove the tea bag.

2 Pour the cooled raspberry leaf tea into a pitcher with the raspberry and orange juices, apple slices, cucumber, and mint leaves. Serve chilled with ice cubes, if using.

68 WATERCRESS

Watercress is a fantastically easy way to add cleansing sulfur, protective antioxidants, and energy-giving chlorophyll to the pregnancy diet.

MAJOR NUTRIENTS PER 25 G/ABOUT 10 SPRIGS WATERCRESS

Calories	3
Total fat	0 g
Protein	0.6 g
Carbohydrate	0.3 g
Fiber	0.1 g
Vitamin C	11 mg
Vitamin A	798 IU
Vitamin E	0.25 mg
Folate	2.25 mcg
Beta-carotene	478 mcg
Lutein/Zeaxanthin	1,442 mcg

Watercress contains the sulfur compounds isothiocyanates. These are very efficient at helping the liver escort out harmful toxins that might otherwise harm the baby. Sulfur helps deliver nutrients and oxygen around the body, aiding its ability to work with vitamin C to produce the collagen that forms the baby's skeleton, muscle, and skin. With vitamins A and E, they enable the mother's skin to stretch while causing minimal damage, and may reduce the baby's future risk of eczema and asthma. The dark green of watercress leaves signifies high levels of the antioxidant carotenoids, beta-carotene, and lutein, which strengthen both mother's and baby's immune system and vision.

• Sulfur eliminates harmful toxins and aids circulation so that oxygen and nutrients can be delivered to the baby.
• Sulfur and vitamins A, C, and E help create the baby's bone, skin, and muscle and the mother's expanding skin.
• May help prevent the baby from developing eczema and asthma.
• Carotenoids beta-carotene and lutein strengthen both mother's and baby's immune systems and vision.

Practical tips:

The darkest green leaves have the most carotenoids and the energizing plant pigment chlorophyll. Choose fresh, open bunches instead of those in sealed bags. Add watercress to meals as you would any salad green. The bitter taste stimulates digestion.

Chile squid with watercress

SERVES 4   (G)(A)(Q)

12 squid tubes and tentacles
(about 1 lb 8 oz), cleaned
and prepared
2–3 tbsp olive oil
1–2 red chiles, seeded
and thinly sliced
2 scallions, finely chopped
lemon wedges, for squeezing,
plus extra to serve
3 good handfuls watercress
2 handfuls baby spinach or arugula
pepper

Dressing

½ cup olive oil
juice of 1 lime
2 shallots, thinly sliced
1 tomato, peeled, seeded,
and finely chopped
1 garlic clove, crushed
pepper

Method

1 To make the dressing, mix together all the ingredients in a bowl, season with pepper to taste, cover, and refrigerate until required.

2 Cut the squid tubes into 2-inch pieces, then score diamond patterns lightly across the flesh with the tip of a sharp knife. Heat the oil in a wok or large skillet over high heat, add the squid pieces and tentacles, and stir-fry for 1 minute. Add the chiles and scallions and stir-fry for an additional minute. Season with pepper to taste and add a good squeeze of lemon juice.

3 Mix the watercress and spinach together, then toss with enough of the dressing to coat lightly. Serve immediately with the squid, together with lemon wedges to squeeze over the squid.

COCONUT WATER

Coconut water is a natural isotonic, with the same electrolyte mineral content as blood plasma. It will naturally hydrate and support the body's higher blood volume.

The electrolyte minerals calcium, magnesium, sodium, and potassium in coconut water are essential to health because they govern electrical impulses and fluid balances in our bodies. They also support the heart as it works 25 percent harder than usual to pump the extra blood. The baby uses up these minerals for the benefit of its own nervous system and fluids, so if the mother does not replenish stocks, she may have deficiency symptoms arising from dehydration, such as muscle cramps, puffiness, fatigue, or headaches. Coconut water is also a good source of energy. The lauric acid it contains destroys bacteria and viruses, and is also found in human breast milk.

- The 40–50 percent increase in blood volume at this time demands higher levels of electrolyte minerals.
- Mother's and baby's muscles, heart, and brain rely on this extra level of hydration and energy.
- Helps prevent electrolyte mineral deficiencies, such as muscle cramps and fatigue.
- Lauric acid protects against viruses and bacteria.

Practical tips:
Coconut water can be siphoned from young, green coconuts. It is also available in cartons. Drink it daily in the run up to the due date to keep the muscles supplied with the minerals it needs for efficient contractions. Coconut water is an ideal energy drink during labor.

DID YOU KNOW?
The sodium in coconut water is an essential mineral, but because modern diets can be too high in sodium chloride, or table salt, it can get out of balance with potassium, commonly low. Here, the two minerals are in the right balance to nourish the baby's kidneys and muscles.

MAJOR NUTRIENTS PER 225 ML/ABOUT 1 CUP COCONUT WATER

Calories	46
Total fat	0.48 g
Lauric acid	211 mg
Protein	1.73 g
Carbohydrate	8.9 g
Fiber	2.6 g
Vitamin C	5.8 mg
Calcium	58 mg
Magnesium	60 mg
Potassium	600 mg
Sodium	252 mg

Fresh coconut juice

SERVES 2   (B)(A)(N)(V)(Q)

2 apples, quartered and cored

1 celery stalk, trimmed, plus 1
  to garnish

3½-inch piece cucumber, quartered
  lengthwise

1 cup coconut water

Method

1 Put the apples, celery, and cucumber in a food processor or blender and process until smooth. Pour into a pitcher, then add the coconut water and stir until combined. Garnish with the celery stalk and serve.

70

BUTTER

Butter provides many components that are crucial to growth, reproduction, and health. It can support increased energy and hormone needs during pregnancy.

There has been a lot of negative press about saturated fats over the past 20 years, but many scientists now believe that they are part of our natural diet and create an important balance with dietary omega-3 and omega-6 fatty acids. Butter provides lecithin, which helps break down fats for absorption so that the baby can use them to make cells. What's more, the sex hormones estrogen and progesterone, produced in very high amounts in the third trimester, can only be made from fats. The butyric acid, myristic acid, and lauric acid in butter are MCTs (medium-chain triglycerides) that fuel your digestive cells to keep in check your defense against bacteria and viruses. We can't store these fats, but use them as dense sources of energy. Lauric acid is also found in human breast milk, a densely fatty substance that the body is now preparing to make.

- Lecithin helps a mother digest crucial fats that can be incorporated into the baby's growing body.
- MCTs support the immune system and digestive function, and can be passed on to the baby.
- Lauric acid and other fats in butter provide the building materials for breast milk.

Practical tips:
Fatigue in pregnancy can occur if there are not enough quality fats in the diet. Butter from grass-fed cows also contains CLA (conjugated linoleic acid), which helps regulate weight.

DID YOU KNOW?

Research has shown that native peoples with diets higher in animal fats from meat have healthier levels of the fat-soluble nutrients, such as the vitamins A, D, and E found in butter, which protect an unborn baby, than vegetarian tribes.

MAJOR NUTRIENTS PER 25 G/2 TBSP BUTTER

Calories	215
Total fat	24.33 g
Monounsaturated fat	6.31 g
Saturated fat	15.4 g
Butyric acid	968 mg
Lauric acid	776 mg
Myristic acid	2,231 mg
Protein	0.26 g
Carbohydrate	0.02 g
Fiber	0 g
Vitamin A	750 IU
Vitamin E	0.7 mg
Vitamin D	18 IU

Broiled halibut with garlic butter

SERVES 4 Ⓖ Ⓑ Ⓐ Ⓠ

6 tbsp butter, plus extra
   for greasing
4 halibut fillets, about 6 oz each,
   rinsed and patted dry
2 garlic cloves, finely chopped
pepper
fresh flat-leaf parsley sprigs,
   to garnish
cooked green beans and lime
   wedges, to serve

Method

1 Preheat the broiler to medium. Grease a shallow, heatproof dish with butter, then arrange the fish in it. Season with pepper.

2 In a separate bowl, mix the butter with the garlic. Arrange pieces of the garlic butter all over the fish, then transfer to the broiler. Cook for 7–8 minutes, turning once, until the fish is cooked through.

3 Remove the dish from the broiler. Using a spatula, remove the fillets from the dish and arrange on individual serving plates. Pour over the remaining melted butter from the dish, and garnish with parsley sprigs. Serve with green beans and lime wedges.

71 PEAS

Peas are a nutritionally dense convenience food. The fiber, zinc, and B vitamins help regulate blood sugar levels to sustain energy in mother and baby.

Iron also supports your energy levels by producing energy in the cells and within muscles, both of which are vital for the baby's rapidly growing body. Dietary protein from plant, as well as animal sources, maintains your body's acid–alkaline balance. A balanced pH ensures that the immune, hormonal, and detoxification systems work optimally and that the kidneys don't become overloaded at a time when they are under pressure from increased blood volume. An increased availability of calcium, which peas can provide, may reduce the body's response to pain during childbirth. Low levels of calcium have been linked to premature births, because tense muscles can cause early uterine contractions.

- Fiber, zinc, iron, and the B vitamins enable constant energy generation to support the baby's growing body.
- Protein helps the body systems work efficiently. The kidneys, in particular, need support because they are dealing with more fluid.
- Contain calcium, which is thought to play a role in regulating pain in labor through decreased nerve responses; tense muscles resulting from calcium deficiency may lead to early labor.

Practical tips:

Always keep a package of peas in the freezer, so that even when you are tired or can't face preparing vegetables, you can add some greenery to your plate. A simple bowl of peas makes a light meal or snack in itself. Add a pat of butter and some pepper to taste.

DID YOU KNOW?

Peas are a legume (bean) rather than a vegetable, which means they are high in protein. They cause less gas in women who find other beans, such as lentils, difficult to digest during pregnancy.

MAJOR NUTRIENTS PER 100 G/⅔ CUP PEAS

Calories	81
Total fat	0.4 g
Protein	5.4 g
Carbohydrate	14.5 g
Fiber	5.1 g
Vitamin C	40 mg
Vitamin B3	2.1 mg
Folate	65 mcg
Calcium	56 mg
Magnesium	33 mg
Potassium	244 mg
Iron	1.5 mg
Zinc	1.2 mg
Lutein/Zeaxanthin	2,477 mcg

Minty pea and bean soup

SERVES 4–6 (G) (A) (V)

1½ tbsp olive oil

*1 bunch scallions, trimmed
    and chopped*

1 large celery stalk, chopped

1 garlic clove, crushed

1 mealy potato, peeled and diced

5 cups vegetable stock

1 bay leaf

1 cup peas

*14 oz of canned flageolet beans,
    drained and rinsed (1½ cups)*

pepper

*finely shredded fresh mint,
    to garnish*

mixed-grain bread rolls, to serve

Method

1 Heat the oil in a large saucepan over medium–high heat. Add the scallions, celery, and garlic and cook, stirring, for about 3 minutes, until soft. Add the potato and stir for an additional minute.

2 Add the stock, bay leaf, and pepper to taste and bring to a boil, stirring. Reduce the heat to low, cover the pan, and simmer for 20 minutes, or until the potatoes are tender. Add the peas and beans and return the soup to a boil.

3 Reduce the heat, cover, and continue to simmer until the peas are tender. Remove and discard the bay leaf, then put the soup into a food processor or blender and process until smooth.

4 Add pepper to taste and reheat. Ladle the soup into warm soup bowls, sprinkle with mint, and serve with bread rolls.

72 GARLIC

Garlic has a long history of use as an antifungal. The regular inclusion of garlic in the diet keeps a check on yeast organisms that can cause thrush.

Vaginal thrush becomes more likely in late pregnancy as estrogen levels reach their peak. This risk is increased if the mother's diet includes a lot of refined sugars. The allicin in garlic is a strong alternative to antifungal medications that can affect beneficial bacteria levels and, therefore, both mother's and baby's immunity. Vaginal thrush can also be passed to the baby during birth or afterward through breast-feeding, causing oral thrush and diaper rash. The potent antioxidants and sulfur compounds in garlic also remove toxins and may help reduce the problems with nasal congestion and breathing that are common in the third trimester. The prebiotic fiber inulin fuels beneficial bacteria, reducing the severity of fungal, bacterial, and viral infections and the likelihood of inflammation and intolerances.

- Antifungal action that doesn't upset natural beneficial bacteria levels and helps stops a mother from passing thrush to the baby.
- Antioxidants and sulfur compounds support immune function and eliminate harmful toxins.
- Prebiotic fiber supports healthy probiotic bacteria levels so that the body can ward off infection.

Practical tips:
Add garlic to cooking but also eat raw, where possible, to obtain its full potency. Garlic needs to be chopped, crushed, or chewed to release the allicin. Add crushed garlic to olive oil.

DID YOU KNOW?

Recent research has found that when garlic was added to the placenta cells of women who either experienced preeclampsia or delivered a baby with a low birth weight, the quality of those cells improved because the enzymes that contribute to both these problems were eliminated.

MAJOR NUTRIENTS PER 2 CLOVES RAW GARLIC

Calories	8
Total fat	0.2 g
Protein	0.38 g
Carbohydrate	0.99 g
Fiber	0.2 g
Vitamin C	0.9 mg

Lemon and garlic spinach

SERVES 4   (A)(N)(V)(Q)

4 tbsp olive oil
2 garlic cloves, thinly sliced
1 lb fresh spinach, torn or shredded
juice of ½ lemon
pepper

Method

1 Heat the oil over high heat in a large skillet. Add the garlic and
spinach and cook, stirring continuously, until the spinach is soft.
Be careful to avoid letting the spinach burn.

2 Remove from the heat, turn into a serving bowl, and sprinkle with
lemon juice. Season with a little pepper. Mix well and serve either
hot or at room temperature.

73 SALMON

Salmon provides protein and antioxidants in support of growth, and the omega-3 fatty acids that are necessary for the health of the joints, eyes, and brain.

DID YOU KNOW?

The DHA and EPA requirements of the baby's brain are so high at this point that if oily fish is absent from the diet, it is advisable to take a fish oil or vegan marine algae DHA supplement.

MAJOR NUTRIENTS PER 100 G/3½ oz WILD SALMON

Calories	142
Total fat	6.34 g
Omega-3 fatty acids—DHA	1.12 g
Omega-3 fatty acids—EPA	0.32 g
Protein	19.9 g
Carbohydrate	0 g
Fiber	0 g
Vitamin B3	7.9 mg
Vitamin B5	1.64 mg
Vitamin B6	0.81 mg
Vitamin B12	2.8 mcg
Vitamin A	40 IU
Vitamin D	435 IU
Choline	94.6 mg
Calcium	12 mg
Magnesium	29 mg
Potassium	490 mg
Phosphorus	200 mg
Selenium	36.5 mcg

Although plant foods, such as walnuts, contain omega-3 fatty acids, our bodies need to convert these before DHA and EPA can be produced. It is easier for the body to obtain the DHA and EPA directly from oily fish, such as salmon. DHA is then immediately incorporated into the hundreds of thousands of new brain and nervous system cells that the baby is producing by the minute. One study found that women with higher DHA levels had babies that were two months ahead developmentally in the first six months of life, although other studies have found no clear link. Vitamins A and D and the B vitamins also support brain function and cognition, including the mother's mood before and after birth. The EPA in salmon supports heart function and makes the substance resolvin that prevents inflammation, which can be a problem in the joints as the body becomes heavier.

• A direct source of the omega-3 fatty acids DHA and EPA.
• DHA supports intense brain growth.
• Vitamins A and D and the B vitamins help support the mother's mood as well as the baby's brain function.
• EPA supports heart function and helps joints stay pain-free.

Practical tips:

Wild salmon has higher levels of omega-3 fatty acids than farmed. These fatty acids can be damaged, so don't overcook. Lightly poach or steam; make sure it is cooked all the way through but is not dry.

Warm salmon and mango salad

SERVES 4   (**G**) (**B**) (**A**)

8 yellow or red cherry tomatoes

2–3 salmon fillets, about 6 oz each,
   skinned and cut into small cubes

1 large ripe mango, peeled and cut
   into small chunks

2 tbsp orange juice

1 tbsp soy sauce

4 handfuls mixed salad greens

½ cucumber, trimmed and sliced
   into batons

6 scallions, trimmed and chopped

Dressing

4 tbsp plain yogurt with live cultures

1 tsp soy sauce

1 tbsp finely grated orange rind

Method

1 Soak 4 wooden skewers in water for 30 minutes. Cut half of the tomatoes in half and set aside. Thread the salmon with the whole tomatoes and half of the mango chunks onto the skewers. Mix the orange juice and soy sauce together in a small bowl and brush over the kebabs. Let marinate for 15 minutes, brushing with the remaining orange juice mixture at least once more.

2 Arrange the salad greens on a serving platter with the remaining halved tomatoes, mango chunks, the cucumber, and scallions.

3 To make the dressing, mix together the yogurt, soy sauce, and grated orange rind in a small bowl and reserve.

4 Preheat the broiler to high and line the broiler rack with foil. Place the salmon kebabs on the broiler rack, brush again with the marinade, and broil for 5–7 minutes, or until the salmon is cooked. Turn the kebabs over halfway through cooking and brush with any remaining marinade.

5 Divide the prepared salad among 4 plates, top each with a kebabs, then drizzle with the dressing.

74

RED BELL PEPPERS

Red bell peppers are one of the richest sources of vitamin C. Vitamin C is the most abundant micronutrient in the body, and the need for it increases during pregnancy.

This is particularly true in the third trimester, when vitamin C is used up quickly to help produce the sex hormones estrogen and progesterone, which maintain pregnancy and prepare the body for birth and breast-feeding. Vitamin C is naturally purged from the body via the urine about twice a day, so it is difficult to have too much of it, and our need is constant. It also supports the collagen production of the baby's rapidly growing body that is necessary for all its structures, including skin, bone, teeth, and muscle. Vitamin C allows for calcium in the diet to be absorbed to make the baby's skeleton and to keep the mother's own bones and teeth from being affected. It also allows for iron to be absorbed and is used to keep blood oxygenated. The vitamin B6 and folate (folic acid) in red bell peppers support healthy brain function and detoxification processes.

- Vitamin C maintains healthy levels of the hormones needed to sustain pregnancy and enable birth and breast-feeding.
- Vitamin C is needed in large amounts for the growth of the baby.
- The absorption of calcium from food relies on vitamin C, as does our utilization of iron for energy.
- Vitamin B6 and folate keep brain and body free of toxins.

Practical tips:
Choose deep red colors to benefit from the fat-protective antioxidant lycopene. Buy with the green stem intact and cut this at the last minute to preserve the vitamin C content.

DID YOU KNOW?

As our primary antioxidant, vitamin C is concentrated in our organs at levels of 10–100 times greater than in the blood. Sufficient levels are vital for the protection of the baby's own organs, including the heart, liver, lungs, and kidneys.

MAJOR NUTRIENTS PER MEDIUM-SIZE RED BELL PEPPER

Calories	37
Total fat	0.36 g
Protein	1.18 g
Carbohydrate	7.18 g
Fiber	2.5 g
Vitamin C	152 mg
Vitamin B6	0.35 mg
Folate	55 mcg

Tomato, lentil, and red bell pepper soup

SERVES 4   (G) (A) (V)

3 tbsp olive oil

2 onions, chopped

2 garlic cloves, chopped

*2 large red bell peppers, seeded
and chopped*

4 ripe tomatoes, chopped

½ cup red split lentils

*2½ cups vegetable stock,
plus extra to thin (optional)*

1 tbsp red wine vinegar

pepper

*2 scallions, chopped, or
1 tbsp snipped fresh chives,
to garnish*

Method

1 Heat the oil in a large saucepan over medium–high heat, add the onions, and cook, stirring, for 5 minutes, or until softened but not browned. Add the garlic and red bell peppers and cook, stirring, for 5 minutes, or until the bell peppers are softened.

2 Add the tomatoes, lentils, and stock and bring to a simmer. Reduce the heat to low, cover, and simmer gently for 25 minutes, or until the lentils are tender. Stir in the vinegar and season with pepper to taste.

3 Let cool slightly, then transfer the soup to a blender or food processor and process for 1 minute, or until smooth. Return to the pan and reheat, stirring in a little hot water or stock if the soup seems a little too thick. Serve in warm soup bowls, garnished with the scallions.

75 ASPARAGUS

Asparagus offers a wealth of supporting nutrients at this demanding stage of pregnancy, when the need for nutrient-dense foods is at its peak.

Asparagus helps provide the nutrients that work together most efficiently in support of the growing baby and the mother's preparation for birth and breast-feeding. Its rich antioxidant profile, which includes vitamins A and E, the minerals selenium and zinc, the carotenoids lutein and beta-carotene, and the flavonoids rutin, quercetin, and kaempferol, protect DNA and maintain both mother's and baby's immune systems. Added to these and enhancing their action is the antioxidant enzyme glutathione. Asparagus is one of a few foods, including onions, garlic, leeks, and bananas, that provide the prebiotic fiber inulin. This fiber enables beneficial digestive bacteria to protect mother and baby from infection. With its antioxidants and the B vitamins, asparagus also helps remove toxins.

- Antioxidant combinations maintain mother's and baby's immune systems and protect DNA.
- The prebiotic fiber inulin supports internal good bacteria, keeping out invaders that may cause infection.
- Antioxidants and the B vitamins enhance the body's ability to tackle harmful toxic buildup that may harm the baby.

Practical tips:
Asparagus can be eaten hot or cold, in salads, stir-fries, as a side dish, or as an appetizer. It works particularly well with lemon or butter or a few Parmesan shavings. Steaming it will retain the most nutrients. The thicker, woodier large stalks contain the most fiber.

DID YOU KNOW?

Asparagus contains vitamin K, which helps both mother's and baby's natural clotting mechanisms, reducing the risk of internal bleeding after delivery.

MAJOR NUTRIENTS PER 10 SPEARS ASPARAGUS

Calories	24
Total fat	0.1 g
Protein	2.64 g
Carbohydrate	4.66 g
Fiber	2.5 g
Vitamin B3	1.17 mg
Vitamin B5	0.33 mg
Vitamin B6	0.11 mg
Vitamin E	1.36 mg
Vitamin A	907 IU
Vitamin K	49.9 mcg
Calcium	29 mg
Magnesium	17 mg
Potassium	242 mg
Zinc	0.65 mg
Selenium	2.8 mcg
Beta-carotene	539 mcg
Lutein/Zeaxanthin	852 mcg

Crispy roasted asparagus

SERVES 4 (**A**) (**Q**)

1 lb asparagus spears, trimmed

2 tbsp extra virgin olive oil

1 tbsp grated Parmesan cheese, to serve

Method

1 Preheat the oven to 400°F.

2 Arrange the asparagus in a single layer on a metal baking sheet. Drizzle with the oil.

3 Place the sheet in the oven and bake for 10–15 minutes, turning once. Remove from the oven, transfer to a dish, and serve immediately, sprinkled with the grated Parmesan.

76 POTATOES

Potatoes can help satisfy the daily need for 200–300 extra calories in this trimester. A meal that includes potatoes can also stop you from craving dessert afterward.

Stress, anxiety, and sleeplessness are common third trimester problems, when the birth is imminent and activity is harder. Potatoes raise serotonin levels in the brain and this sleep and mood neurotransmitter (brain chemical) promotes relaxation and quality sleep. The vitamins B6 and C in potatoes aids this action and also ensures that energy is released from food at the right times, making it easier to cope with the day. Vitamin B6 is a very important pregnancy nutrient. It makes possible the use of iron, it breaks down and makes use of protein for growth, it draws energy from carbohydrate foods, and it regulates the pregnancy hormones. The vitamin C in potato protects the baby's vulnerable brain and nerve cells as they rapidly develop.

- Potatoes are naturally calming, promoting sleep.
- Vitamins B6 and C help release energy from food and produce serotonin to regulate mood and sleep.
- Vitamin B6 plays an important role in hormonal, growth, and energy processes in pregnancy.
- Vitamin C protects the baby's sensitive brain cells.

Practical tips:
Choose new potatoes in their skins to get the most fiber and to benefit from the nutrients that are concentrated under the skin. Older potatoes are far more sugary and have a less positive effect on energy and mood.

DID YOU KNOW?

Chemicals called kukoamines in potatoes work with vitamins C and B6 and the potassium also present to help lower blood pressure, a vital task at a time of increased blood volume and physical stress.

MAJOR NUTRIENTS PER 100 G/ABOUT 1 MEDIUM-SIZE POTATO

Calories	77
Total fat	0.1 g
Protein	2 g
Carbohydrate	19 g
Fiber	2.2 g
Vitamin C	20 mg
Vitamin B6	0.25 mg
Potassium	421 mg

Potato and tomato tortilla

SERVES 6   (G)(B)(A)(V)(Q)

9 potatoes (about 2 lb 4 oz), peeled
    and cut into small cubes

2 tbsp olive oil

1 bunch scallions, chopped

8 cherry tomatoes

6 eggs

3 tbsp water

2 tbsp chopped fresh parsley

pepper

Method

1 Cook the potatoes in a saucepan of boiling water for 8–10 minutes, or until tender. Drain and reserve until required.

2 Preheat the broiler to medium. Heat the oil in a large, ovenproof skillet, add the scallions and fry until just soft. Add the potatoes and fry for 3–4 minutes, until coated with oil and hot. Smooth the top and scatter over the tomatoes.

3 Mix the eggs, water, pepper, and parsley together in a bowl, then pour into the skillet. Cook over gentle heat for 10–15 minutes, until the tortilla looks fairly set.

4 Place the skillet under the hot broiler and cook until the top of the tortilla is brown and set. Let stand to cool for 10–15 minutes before sliding out of the skillet onto a cutting board. Cut into wedges and serve immediately.

77 CASHEW NUTS

Cashew nuts are often overlooked in favor of other nuts, but they have excellent levels of the same heart-protective monounsaturated fats found in olive oil.

At this stage, the mother's heart is working 25 percent harder than usual to pump the extra blood around the body, while the baby's heart is just starting its life, so both need a lot of nutritional support. Studies have shown that the monounsaturated fat, oleic acid, enables the heart to use oxygen and fuel more efficiently. The minerals calcium, magnesium, and potassium in cashew nuts also encourage two strong heartbeats, while the B vitamins ensure energy is released completely into every cell. These minerals also regulate nerve and muscle function. One molecule of calcium is needed for every muscle contraction during labor and magnesium helps strengthen muscles in the uterus. These two "calming minerals" also help relieve stress, and promote relaxation and sleep.

- Oleic acid protects mother's and baby's hearts and helps them to work effectively.
- Calcium, magnesium, potassium, and the B vitamins keep heartbeats strong.
- Calcium and magnesium keep the nervous system calm and prepare the muscles for birth contractions.

DID YOU KNOW?

The antioxidant and energy nutrient coenzyme Q-10 is found in meat and fish, but cashew nuts are a good vegetarian source. It may help prevent preeclampsia and aid contractions.

MAJOR NUTRIENTS PER 25 G/ABOUT 18 CASHEW NUTS

Calories	166
Total fat	13.15 g
Monounsaturated fat	7.14 g
Saturated fat	2.34 g
Omega-6 fatty acids	2,335 mg
Protein	5.47 g
Carbohydrate	9.06 g
Fiber	1 g
Vitamin B3	0.32 mg
Vitamin B5	0.26 mg
Vitamin B6	0.125 mg
Calcium	11 mg
Magnesium	88 mg
Potassium	198 mg
Phosphorus	178 mg
Iron	2.0 mg
Zinc	1.73 mg
Manganese	0.50 mg

Practical tips:
Cashew nuts make excellent nut butter, simply blended on their own. If used in cooking, they should be added only at the very end to avoid damaging the omega-6 fatty acids. For this reason, choose raw cashew nuts to snack on instead of roasted.

Cashew nut paella

SERVES 4   (G) (B) (A) (V)

2 tbsp olive oil

1 tbsp butter

1 red onion, chopped

¾ cup risotto rice

1 tsp turmeric

1 tsp ground cumin

3 garlic cloves, crushed

1 red bell pepper, seeded and
*   diced (optional)*

6 baby corn, halved lengthwise

2 tbsp pitted black olives

1 large tomato, seeded
*   and diced*

2 cups vegetable stock

⅔ cup unsalted cashew nuts

⅓ cup frozen peas

2 tbsp chopped fresh flat-leaf
*   parsley, plus extra to garnish*

pinch of cayenne pepper

pepper

Method

1 Heat the oil and butter in a large skillet or paella pan until the butter has melted.

2 Add the onion and cook over medium heat, stirring continuously, for 2–3 minutes, until softened.

3 Stir in the rice, turmeric, cumin, garlic, red bell pepper, if using, baby corn, olives, and tomato and cook over medium heat, stirring occasionally, for 1–2 minutes.

4 Pour in the stock and bring the mixture to a boil. Reduce the heat and cook gently, stirring continuously, for an additional 20 minutes.

5 Add the cashew nuts and peas and continue to cook, stirring occasionally, for another 5 minutes. Season to taste with pepper and add the parsley and a pinch of cayenne pepper. Transfer the paella to warm serving plates and garnish with extra parsley.

78

BUTTERNUT SQUASH

Butternut squash is an energy-supporting vegetable that also contains a wide range of antioxidants to help reduce inflammation, pain, infection, and cell damage.

Taking on board high levels of antioxidants from a range of foods, including squash, ensures that the damage to your body caused by certain elements, such as pollution, chemicals, medications, and sunlight is limited. The effects can be heightened in the third trimester when added exertion raises stress levels. The vitamins A and C in squash support the fatty and watery parts of the body respectively, and ensure the health of your mucous membranes, helping to relieve any nasal congestion and breathing issues. Protecting these membranes also helps both mother and baby fight infection. The trace mineral manganese in squash provides additional protection from illness by helping to produce the antioxidant enzyme superoxide dismutase (SOD). Manganese also helps the body absorb calcium and create new bone and cartilage.

- Contains antioxidants that protect both mother and baby from environmental and internal stress factors.
- Vitamins A and C support the mucous membranes to reduce nasal problems and fight infection.
- Manganese produces the antioxidant enzyme SOD and supports healthy bone and cartilage growth.

Practical tips:
Use butternut squash as you would any root vegetable. Or simply cut in half, drizzle with olive oil, and roast. Butternut squash soup is an easily digested energy source.

DID YOU KNOW?

Calcium and magnesium are needed in a ratio of around 3:2 for both to work in the body. We tend to get more calcium than magnesium in our diets, via dairy foods and water, but squash offers a good balance of the two.

MAJOR NUTRIENTS PER 100 G/3½ OZ (ABOUT ¾ CUP CUBES) SQUASH

Calories	45
Total fat	0.1 g
Protein	1 g
Carbohydrate	11.69 g
Fiber	2 g
Vitamin C	21 mg
Vitamin A	10,630 IU
Calcium	48 mg
Magnesium	34 mg
Potassium	352 mg
Manganese	0.2 mg

Roasted butternut squash

SERVES 4   Ⓖ Ⓐ

1 small butternut squash

1 onion, chopped

2–3 garlic cloves, crushed

4 small tomatoes, chopped

1½ cups chopped cremini
mushrooms

3 oz of canned lima beans, drained,
rinsed, and coarsely chopped
(about ⅓ cup)

1 zucchini, trimmed and grated

1 tbsp chopped fresh oregano,
plus extra to garnish

2 tbsp tomato paste

1¼ cups water

4 scallions, trimmed and chopped

1 tbsp Worcestershire or hot
pepper sauce, or to taste

pepper

Method

1 Preheat the oven to 375°F. Prick the squash all over with a metal skewer, then roast for 40 minutes, or until tender. Remove from the oven and let stand until cool enough to handle.

2 Cut the squash in half, scoop out and discard the seeds, then scoop out some of the flesh, making hollows in both halves. Chop the scooped-out flesh and put in a bowl. Place the two halves side by side in a large roasting pan.

3 Add the onion, garlic, chopped tomatoes, and mushrooms to the squash flesh in the bowl. Add the lima beans, zucchini, oregano, and a little pepper to taste, and mix well. Spoon the filling into the 2 halves of the squash, packing it down as firmly as possible.

4 Mix the tomato paste with the water, scallions, and Worcestershire sauce in a small bowl and pour around the squash.

5 Cover loosely with a large sheet of foil and bake for 30 minutes, or until piping hot. Serve in warm bowls, garnished with oregano.

79 BLUEBERRIES

The deep color of blueberries indicates their high levels of proanthocyanidins. These support circulation, a crucial factor in late pregnancy.

With an extra 40–50 percent of blood flowing around the body, it is imperative that the blood vessels stay intact and strong. Proanthocyanidins help with this, along with the vitamins C and A that are also present in blueberries. Easy bruising, varicose veins, nosebleeds, and hemorrhoids are common symptoms that result from damage to blood vessels. Effective circulation also ensures good skin condition, brain function, and a steady supply of oxygen and nutrients to the placenta and baby; any break in the flow can be detrimental. Proanthocyanidins are also believed to neutralize the enzymes that cause inflammation and can damage connective tissue, relieving pregnancy aches and pains, including discomfort in the joints, carpal tunnel, and pelvic girdle pain.

- Provide proanthocyanidin circulatory support to help prevent hemorrhoids, varicose veins, and easy bruising.
- Healthy blood flow ensures the baby receives a constant supply of oxygen and nutrients.
- A naturally anti-inflammatory food that helps relieve common pregnancy symptoms, including joint pains.

Practical tips:
Blueberries can be easily frozen and enjoyed whenever convenient, either as a snack or in smoothies or yogurt. They are a perfect food to graze on during labor because they are digested quickly and will help keep oxygen flowing to the contracting muscles.

DID YOU KNOW?

Blueberries and other strong antioxidant foods support the production of your immune antibodies. These are able to pass through the placenta and give protection directly to the baby.

MAJOR NUTRIENTS PER 100 G/ABOUT ⅔ CUP BLUEBERRIES

Calories	57
Total fat	0.33 g
Protein	0.74 g
Carbohydrate	14.49 g
Fiber	2.4 g
Vitamin C	9.7 mg
Vitamin A	54 IU
Lutein/Zeaxanthin	80 mcg

Blueberry nectar

SERVES 1–2 (A) (V) (Q)

1 pear, peeled and cored

1 cup blueberries

½ cup plain yogurt with live cultures

½ tsp honey

2 tsp slivered almonds

Method

1 Put the pear and blueberries into a food processor or blender. Add the yogurt and honey and process until smooth and frothy. Pour into glasses, sprinkle with the almonds, and serve.

5

Postnatal Nutrition

Postnatal nutrition is all about recovery, healing, and helping you cope with the aftereffects of birth. Bringing down inflammation and preventing infection around the birth area is an obvious priority, but pain relief, ease of bowel movements, and milk flow can also be helped by dietary factors.

Good-quality, sustaining foods help support energy and mood, and provide you with vital antidepressant nutrients, such as zinc, the B vitamins, and magnesium. If breast-feeding, this is doubly important, because your recovery and health can be affected as you provide your baby with the nutrients it needs to thrive and grow. Milk production can require as much as 500 extra calories a day in energy, and that needs to come from nutrient-dense food.

(G) Growth of baby
(B) Brain development of baby
(A) Immunity-supporting antioxidants
(N) Natural remedy
(V) Suitable for vegetarians
(Q) Quick and easy to prepare

80

FENNEL

Fennel contains phytoestrogens, which means that it supports the hormones that maintain healthy milk supply. Foods that can do this are called galactogogues.

Foods that are high in phytoestrogens, such as soy, are not recommended after birth, but the levels in fennel provide gentle and balanced support without overloading the baby's delicate hormones. The antioxidants in fennel also help prevent infections, making this an excellent recovery food. The vitamin C content, along with the bioflavonoids rutin and quercetin, work hard to keep the blood vessels intact, helping to calm post-birth bleeding, encourage wound healing, and prevent hemorrhoids. These nutrients are also anti-inflammatory, so they help to relieve swelling and discomfort, while the vitamin C in combination with the sulfur in fennel produces collagen, promoting the healing of all the body's tissues. Fennel has been used traditionally to treat digestive complaints, such as gas and bloating, to help shed excess fluid, and to regulate blood pressure, all of which may be problems after birth.

- A galactagogue food, traditionally used to bring on milk supply.
- Antioxidants vitamin C, quercetin, and rutin help prevent infections, reduce inflammation, and support healing.
- Vitamin C and sulfur help healing through collagen generation.
- Supports digestion, fluid, and blood pressure regulation post-birth.

DID YOU KNOW?

Fennel seeds have a long tradition of use in postnatal recovery. Mothers across the world drink fennel seed tea both to boost milk production and to relieve stomach complaints, whether in themselves or the baby.

MAJOR NUTRIENTS PER HALF BULB FENNEL

Calories	36.5
Total fat	0.24 g
Protein	1.45 g
Carbohydrate	8.53 g
Fiber	3.65 g
Vitamin C	14.1 mg
Folate	31.5 mcg
Potassium	484.5 mg

Practical tips:

Sliced raw fennel adds a pleasing, fresh anise taste to salads. It can also be braised and served as a side dish, added to soups, or included in juices to boost their cleansing power.

Salmon and fennel salad

SERVES 2

6 new potatoes, scrubbed

2 skinless salmon fillets, about
    4 oz each

½ small head butterhead lettuce

1 handful baby spinach leaves

¾ cup thinly sliced fennel

1 cooked beet, diced

2 tbsp diced red onion

1½-inch piece cucumber, seeded
    and diced

Dressing

6 tbsp sour cream

2 tbsp lemon juice

1 tbsp snipped fresh chives

4 fresh dill sprigs, fronds chopped

1 tbsp extra virgin olive oil

1 tbsp water

pepper

Method

1 Line the broiler rack with foil and preheat the broiler to high. Cook the potatoes in boiling water for 10 minutes, or until tender; drain and set aside.

2 Broil the salmon for 6–8 minutes, depending on the thickness of the fillets, turning once, until cooked.

3 Meanwhile, divide the lettuce and spinach between two plates. Top with the fennel, beet, onion, and cucumber. Mix together the ingredients for the dressing.

4 Either top the salad with the whole salmon fillets or flake the fish and place on top. Drizzle the dressing over before serving.

81

WALNUTS

Walnuts supply some of the extra energy a mother needs to look after a new baby, while also encouraging healing and recovery after birth.

MAJOR NUTRIENTS PER 25 G/1 oz WALNUTS

Calories	196
Total fat	19.5 g
Monounsaturated fat	2.68 g
Omega-3 fatty acids	2,728 mg
Omega-6 fatty acids	11,428 mg
Omega-9 fatty acids	2,639 mg
Protein	4.57 g
Carbohydrate	4.1 g
Fiber	2 g
Vitamin B3	0.34 mg
Vitamin B5	0.17 mg
Vitamin B6	0.16 mg
Magnesium	47.4 mg
Potassium	132 mg
Manganese	1.02 mg
Selenium	1.47 mcg
Zinc	0.93 mg
Phytosterols	32.4 mg

The mixture of beneficial oils, good-quality protein, and complex carbohydrates in walnuts help to keep up energy, mood, and milk supply at this time. The effectiveness is accentuated by the B-vitamin, zinc, magnesium, and manganese content. A lot of protein is supplied to the baby in breast milk, so a mother's healing can be reduced if her dietary intake is low. Walnuts are a natural mood food because they are instrumental in producing the "happy" brain chemical serotonin. The hormone melatonin, present in walnuts, helps us fall asleep easily and sleep well when we do—when your sleep is being broken on a nightly basis, quality is essential.

- Contain balanced carbohydrates, protein, and fats, supplying sustained energy for milk supply and a demanding schedule.
- The B vitamins, zinc, magnesium, and manganese allow for the best possible energy to be obtained from all the foods you eat.
- Protein and nutrients encourage serotonin production, helping to combat any postnatal depression.
- The hormone melatonin enables a new mother to snatch the best-quality sleep when she can.

Practical tips:

Snack on raw, unsalted walnuts when breast-feeding or looking after the baby to promote good blood sugar balance and to avoid energy lows. This will also help to keep calorie intake regular, ensuring a consistent milk supply.

Bean and walnut salad

SERVES 2 Ⓖ Ⓐ Ⓠ

4 cups green beans
1 small onion, finely chopped
1 garlic clove, chopped
¼ cup freshly grated Parmesan
　cheese
2 tbsp chopped walnuts, to garnish

Dressing

2 tbsp cider vinegar
6 tbsp olive oil
2 tsp chopped fresh tarragon

Method

1 Bring a large saucepan of water to a boil, add the beans, and cook for 5 minutes, or until just tender. Remove with a slotted spoon and refresh the beans under cold running water. Drain and put into a mixing bowl, then add the onion, garlic, and cheese.

2 To make the dressing, put all the ingredients in a small screw-top jar and shake until well blended. Pour over the salad, cover with plastic wrap, and chill for at least 30 minutes.

3 Remove the salad from the refrigerator, give it a quick stir, and transfer to serving dishes. Sprinkle the walnuts over the salad and serve.

82 BANANAS

Bananas provide good levels of potassium, the mineral needed for fluid balance and to enable the muscle contractions that shrink the uterus back to normal size.

A breast-fed baby will take large amounts of its mother's potassium for its developing nervous system and muscles. A mother who is left deficient may have headaches, fatigue, or muscle cramps. Bananas also deliver a healthy dose of vitamin C, which along with the tryptophan and vitamin B6, helps to lift mood, promote sleep, and combat postnatal depression. These nutrients also encourage regular and easy bowel movements at a time when hemorrhoids are common. As well as softening stools, the fiber inulin in bananas helps keep the body's beneficial probiotic bacteria at healthy levels. This is vital for immune health during recovery, and for keeping infection at bay.

- High potassium content supplies a mother's needs and is also required in breast milk for the baby's brain and muscle function.
- Vitamins C and B6 and tryptophan help produce serotonin for good mood and sleep.
- Support healthy bowel movements to help prevent hemorrhoids.
- Contain the fiber inulin, which promotes healthy digestive bacteria for immune health and the prevention of infection.

Practical tips:
Bananas with raw nuts are the perfect snack because the added protein slows down the sugar release of the bananas. Bananas that are less ripe release their sugars into the bloodstream more slowly, supplying a more controlled form of energy.

DID YOU KNOW?
Bananas are used by athletes to maintain energy levels as they push their bodies to extremes. A new mother, facing similar demands, can boost her energy in the same way.

MAJOR NUTRIENTS PER MEDIUM-SIZE BANANA

Calories	105
Total fat	0.39 g
Protein	1.29 g
Fiber	3.1 g
Carbohydrate	26.95 g
Vitamin C	10.3 mg
Vitamin B6	0.43 mg
Potassium	422 mg
Tryptophan	11 mg

Indian rice pudding with banana

SERVES 2 (**B**) (**A**) (**V**)

½ cup brown rice

1½ cups milk

3 cardamom pods, split

1 cup water

1 tsp ground cinnamon, plus extra
  to serve

1 tsp vanilla bean paste or extract

heaping 1 tbsp honey, plus extra
  to serve

finely grated zest of 1 small orange

1 large banana, sliced

1 tbsp slivered almonds

Method

1 Put the rice in a heavy-bottom saucepan with the milk, cardamom, and water. Bring to a boil, then reduce the heat to the lowest setting and simmer, covered, for 25–30 minutes, until the rice is tender (there should still be some liquid in the pan).

2 Remove from the heat, stir in the cinnamon, vanilla, honey, and orange zest and let stand, covered, for 5 minutes.

3 Spoon the rice into serving bowls and top with the banana and almonds. Sprinkle with extra cinnamon and drizzle with honey before serving.

83 SWEET POTATO

Sweet potatoes help strengthen immunity. Including them in the diet when breast-feeding results in more disease-attacking antibodies being passed to the baby.

Sweet potatoes provide calcium in balance with magnesium, enabling these two minerals to work at their most efficient in our bones and nervous system. We often receive these minerals in unbalanced amounts; dairy foods, for example, are high in calcium but relatively low in magnesium. While breast-feeding, the body's mineral levels need to be as high as during pregnancy, because the baby will take calcium in breast milk for use in bone development. If you have known problems with bone or tooth density, it is especially important to keep up your calcium levels. Even a nonbreast-feeding mother may have lost calcium bone stores while pregnant. Sweet potatoes are also an excellent source of the antioxidant beta-carotene, which will help rid the body of harmful toxins. The vitamin C content also helps provide collagen, which contributes to bone mass.

- Provides calcium in balance with magnesium for the most effective support to bone growth.
- Calcium is needed in breast milk for the baby's bone growth; if it doesn't come from the diet, it is taken from the mother's bones.
- Vitamin C helps generate collagen, which supports bone structure.

Practical tips:
Use in the same way as white potatoes or any root vegetable. Eat sweet potatoes with a little oil, such as olive oil or butter, because this will enable your body to absorb their fat-soluble nutrients.

DID YOU KNOW?

Calcium and magnesium are called the "calming minerals" because they reduce anxiety and help us relax and fall asleep. They are especially important at a time when the body needs to conserve energy for recovery.

MAJOR NUTRIENTS PER 100 G/ABOUT 1 SMALL SWEET POTATO

Calories	86
Total fat	trace
Protein	1.6 g
Carbohydrate	20.1 g
Fiber	3 g
Vitamin C	2.4 mg
Vitamin E	0.27 mg
Calcium	30 mg
Magnesium	25.3 mg
Potassium	337.3 mg
Iron	0.6 mg
Selenium	0.6 mcg
Beta-carotene	8,506.7 mcg

Baked sweet potatoes with ginger

SERVES 4 （**G**）（**A**）（**V**）

4 sweet potatoes
vegetable oil, for brushing
4 tbsp butter
1-inch piece fresh ginger, sliced
  into very thin matchsticks
2 tbsp chopped fresh cilantro
pepper

Method

1 Preheat the oven to 450°F. Brush the sweet potatoes with oil and bake in the preheated oven for 40–45 minutes, until tender. Cut a cross in the top of each potato. Press the flesh upward until it bursts through the cuts.

2 Heat the butter in a skillet over medium–high heat until foaming. Add the ginger and cook for 3–4 minutes, until golden and crisp.

3 Pour the ginger-and-butter mixture over the potatoes. Sprinkle with the cilantro, season with pepper to taste, and serve.

84 APRICOTS

Apricots help maintain bowel regularity. Pectin, the fiber in apricots, helps soften stools and remove toxins that may enter breast milk from the body.

After childbirth, bowel movements are not always easy and the problem can be exacerbated by dehydration. It is particularly important to obtain plenty of water from vegetables and fruits, such as apricots, because their natural sugars will help to draw water into the body cells. The beta-carotene content in apricots is converted to vitamin A by the body, which heals and strengthens skin that has been torn, cut, or stretched. It is also needed in breast milk for the baby's immune system and the development of his or her sight, taste, and hearing. Vitamin A, along with the vitamin C content of apricots, is needed to utilize iron to take oxygen to tissues that require healing, and to replace any blood lost during childbirth.

- Help ease bowel movements, and, therefore, eliminate toxins, through good hydration and the fiber pectin.
- Vitamin A helps heal skin after pregnancy and childbirth.
- Vitamin A content in breast milk supports the baby's immunity and sensory abilities.
- Vitamins A and C enable iron to oxygenate the blood for healing and to replace any blood loss.

DID YOU KNOW?

Do not buy dried apricots containing the preservative sulfur dioxide. It can cause digestive discomfort, as well as headaches and asthma, and may pass into breast milk.

MAJOR NUTRIENTS PER 3 DRIED APRICOTS

Calories	47
Total fat	trace
Protein	1.2 g
Carbohydrate	10.8 g
Fiber	1.9 g
Vitamin C	trace
Potassium	414 mg
Iron	1 mg
Beta-carotene	163 mcg

Practical tips:
Make into a puree by blending with boiling water. Keep in the refrigerator for a few days as a healthy sweetener for oatmeal, yogurt, and cereal. Add cinnamon to enable the slow-release sugars to work even more effectively.

Apricot crisp

SERVES 6 (G) (A) (N) (V)

unsalted butter, for greasing
1 lb 2 oz fresh apricots, pitted
    and sliced
2 tbsp water
1 tsp ground cinnamon
Greek-style yogurt, to serve

Crumbly topping

1½ cups whole wheat flour
3 tbsp unsalted butter
¼ cup packed brown sugar
½ cup finely chopped hazelnuts

Method

1 Preheat the oven to 400°F. Grease a 5-cup ovenproof dish with
   a little unsalted butter.
2 To make the crumbly topping, put the flour in a bowl and rub in the
   unsalted butter. Stir in the sugar and then the hazelnuts.
3 Arrange the apricots in the bottom of the prepared dish and add the
   water and cinnamon. Sprinkle the crumbly topping evenly over the
   fruit until it is covered. Transfer to the preheated oven and bake for
   about 25 minutes, until golden. Serve hot with Greek-style yogurt.

85 LENTILS

Hearty foods, such as lentils, help a new mother to lose her pregnancy weight safely. They provide constant energy at a time when restricting food is ill-advised.

MAJOR NUTRIENTS PER 100 G/ABOUT ½ CUP DRIED LENTILS

Calories	353
Total fat	1.06 g
Protein	25.8 g
Carbohydrate	60.08 g
Fiber	30.5 g
Vitamin B1	0.87 mg
Vitamin B2	0.21 mg
Vitamin B3	2.61 mg
Vitamin B5	2.14 mg
Vitamin B6	0.54 mg
Folate	479 mcg
Magnesium	122 mg
Iron	7.54 mg
Manganese	1.33 mg
Selenium	8.3 mcg
Zinc	4.78 mg

When recovering from birth, and while breast-feeding, prioritizing the high energy needs of these processes is more important than worrying about losing the weight gained during pregnancy. The B vitamins, zinc, fiber, complex carbohydrates, and protein in lentils help their energy to be released extremely efficiently, resulting in steady blood sugar balance. The zinc content of lentils also supports wound healing and immunity. If breast-feeding, the iron and folate (folic acid) will help to keep the baby's blood circulating. The magnesium and folate in lentils are also needed for brain and nerve function.

- Dense nutritional package that supports sustained energy for healing, recuperation, and breast milk production.
- Consistent supply of slow-release energy prevents cravings for sugary foods with low nutrient content.
- Contain zinc for immune system support and healing.
- Contain iron and folate for the baby's blood.
- Contain magnesium and folate for the development of the baby's nervous system.

Practical tips:

A breast-feeding mother who tends to have gas after eating lentils may find this affects the baby, too. Lentils can be more easily digested if soaked overnight. Throw away the soaking water with its problematic starches before cooking.

Vegetable and lentil casserole

SERVES 4   (G)(B)(A)(V)

3 cloves
1 onion, peeled but left whole
1 cup Puy or green lentils
1 bay leaf
6 cups vegetable stock
2 leeks, sliced
2 potatoes, diced
2 carrots, chopped
3 zucchini, sliced
1 celery stalk, chopped
*1 red bell pepper, seeded
    and chopped*
1 tbsp lemon juice
pepper

Method

1 Preheat the oven to 350°F. Press the cloves into the onion. Put
   the lentils into a large casserole dish, then add the onion and bay
   leaf and pour in the stock. Cover and cook in the preheated oven
   for 1 hour.

2 Remove the onion and discard the cloves. Slice the onion and
   return it to the casserole dish with the vegetables. Stir thoroughly
   and season with pepper to taste. Cover and return to the oven
   for 1 hour.

3 Remove and discard the bay leaf. Stir in the lemon juice and serve
   straight from the casserole dish.

86 ALFALFA

Sprouting seeds, such as alfalfa sprouts, contain all the nutrients needed for the most important growing phase in a young plant's life. Humans need these, too.

The perfect amino acid (protein) content of alfalfa helps wounds heal, keeps toxins out of breast milk, and helps prevent or clear up any infections that can occur after childbirth. Meanwhile, the antioxidants vitamins A and C and beta-carotene support immune function and help the body to repair itself efficiently. In many traditional medicines, alfalfa is prescribed to improve the quality and flow of breast milk because of its action as a mild phytoestrogen food. It is also used for soothing digestive complaints because its enzymes can help break down food to relieve gas and constipation, which may add to postpartum hemorrhoids and pain. In addition, alfalfa is a rich source of the energizing and detoxifying plant pigment chlorophyll.

- Good-quality protein content promotes healing, healthy breast milk, and our ability to fight infection.
- Alkalizing and antioxidant-rich food that helps bring down inflammation, repair wounds, and relieve pain.
- Traditional galactagogue, promoting healthy milk flow.
- Digestive aid that eases gas, constipation, and hemorrhoids.

Practical tips:
Sprinkle on salads or in sandwiches and wraps to add a fresh taste and crunchy texture. Alfalfa can be bought already sprouted at health food stores or supermarkets or grown at home. If eating during pregnancy, cook alfalfa thoroughly.

DID YOU KNOW?

Alfalfa, and other plant foods, can provide a good amount of our daily water needs. Dehydration while breast-feeding can result in a poor uptake of the water-soluble B vitamins and vitamin C in breast milk.

MAJOR NUTRIENTS PER 40 G/ABOUT 1 CUP ALFALFA

Calories	9.2
Total fat	0.28 g
Protein	1.60 g
Carbohydrate	0.84 g
Fiber	0.76 g
Vitamin C	3.28 mg
Vitamin A	62 IU
Vitamin B3	0.19 mg
Vitamin B5	0.22 mg
Vitamin K	30.5 mcg
Choline	5.76 mg
Beta-carotene	34.8 mcg
Calcium	12.8 mg
Magnesium	10.8 mg

Rice paper bundles with alfalfa

MAKES 8   (G)(A)(N)(V)(Q)

1 oz rice vermicelli noodles
8 dried rice paper wrappers
2½ oz thinly sliced, cooked
    chicken breast
2 scallions, shredded
1½-inch piece cucumber, quartered
    lengthwise, seeded, and thinly
    sliced
handful alfalfa
3 tbsp chopped fresh basil
3 tbsp chopped fresh mint

Dipping sauce
2 tbsp fish sauce
1 tbsp light soy sauce
juice of ½ lime
½ tsp light brown sugar
½ tsp dried chile flakes

Method

1. To make the dipping sauce, mix together all the ingredients in a small bowl.
2. Put the noodles in a bowl and cover with boiling water. Stir to separate the noodles, cover, and let stand for about 4 minutes, or according to package directions, until tender. Drain then refresh under cold running water; set aside.
3. Fill a large bowl with hot water. Dunk a rice paper wrapper into the water, let stand for a few seconds, until soft and pliable, then lift out and lay flat on a work surface—be careful because they tear easily.
4. Arrange one-eighth of the noodles down the center of the wrapper, leaving space at the sides. Top with a few pieces of chicken, scallion, cucumber, alfalfa, basil, and mint, then fold in the sides of the wrapper and roll up to make a bundle. Continue, making 8 bundles in total. Serve with the dipping sauce.

87 FENUGREEK

Fenugreek is a useful food for women who are having difficulty breast-feeding. It has a long history in many cultures as a galactagogue, or milk-promoting substance.

Fenugreek and various other foods, including alfalfa, dill, fennel, and asparagus, are all known galactagogues. Including some of them in the diet will encourage milk supply and quality when there are problems. Fenugreek is also good at balancing blood sugar levels, which means it levels out highs and lows of energy. It contains potent levels of several antioxidants, including apigenin, rutin, and quercetin. Some studies have even shown that it boosts levels of other antioxidants in the body, helping to prevent damage to our body tissues. When included as part of a healthy diet, it will help provide energy to cells for healing and bring down inflammation, speeding the recovery process and relieving pain. Fenugreek may also help reduce excess mucus, so it may help to clear up any nasal congestion or digestive problems hanging around after pregnancy.

• Promotes good-quality milk supply in breast-feeding mothers.
• Helps balance blood sugar levels for sustained energy.
• Antioxidant mix heals and soothes inflamed tissues.
• Helps reduce mucus to relieve nasal and digestive problems.

Practical tips:
To boost lactation, fenugreek is typically taken as a tea. Capsules or tinctures can be taken under the guidance of a qualified herbalist. Fenugreek may interact with some medications, and can also cause problems in women with asthma, allergies, or diabetes, so first check with your health-care provider before consuming.

DID YOU KNOW?

Fenugreek contains a compound called trigonelline, a potent antioxidant known to help stimulate the regeneration of brain cells. This is what gives fenugreek (and coffee) its pungent bitter taste.

MAJOR NUTRIENTS PER 15 G/1 TBSP FENUGREEK SEEDS

Calories	36
Total fat	0.71 g
Protein	2.55 g
Carbohydrate	6.48 g
Fiber	2.7 g
Calcium	20 mg
Magnesium	21 mg
Potassium	85 mg
Phosphorus	33 mg
Iron	3.72 mg

Fenugreek tea

SERVES 2 (A)(N)(V)(Q)

2½ cups water
2 tsp fenugreek seeds
1 tsp honey (optional)
ice cubes and lemon slices,
    to serve (optional)

Method

1 Pour the water into a saucepan and bring to a boil. Add the seeds and boil for 5 minutes.

2 Remove from the heat and let steep for 10–15 minutes.

3 Strain and pour into two cups, adding honey to taste, if using. The tea can also be served as a refreshing cold drink with ice cubes and a slice of lemon.

88 DILL

Dill is a galactagogue herb, so it promotes both the volume and quality of breast milk, helping a new mother deliver vital nutrients to her baby.

Even if a baby is only breast-fed for a short time, dill in the mother's diet can help provide it with vital vitamin A, which is known to be lower in exclusively bottle-fed babies. Vitamin A helps prevent infectious disease. Babies with low levels of this vitamin have been known to have poor growth, eye problems, and diarrhea. Dill is also an antibacterial agent, helping prevent the spread of infection in the mother that can hinder recovery and may affect the baby. Including as many calcium- and magnesium-rich foods as possible in the diet is particularly important if bones and teeth are affected during pregnancy. The vitamins A, C, and B3 are also needed to keep up the mother's own bone mass.

- A galactagogue, promoting a good flow of healthy breast milk.
- Vitamin A ensures good levels in breast milk for the baby's health.
- Antibacterial agent that helps keep down the proliferation of infectious bacteria.
- Rich in bone and teeth-strengthening vitamins and minerals for both mother and breast-fed baby.

Practical tips:
Dill has a delicate anise flavor, and it can be added to everyday foods such as eggs, cottage cheese, potato salad, and smoked salmon. Mix it with butter to add an extra dimension to crackers and toast. Make dill tea from the seeds or leaves to help calm an upset stomach and encourage sleep.

DID YOU KNOW?

Dill is the main ingredient in traditional herbal gripe waters for colicky babies. In India, mothers use a tea made from a mix of ajwain (carom seeds), cumin, fennel, and dill weed.

MAJOR NUTRIENTS PER 15 G/12 SPRIGS DILL

Calories	12.9
Total fat	0.2 g
Protein	0.52 g
Carbohydrate	1.05 g
Fiber	0.3 g
Vitamin C	12.8 mg
Vitamin B3	0.24 mg
Vitamin A	1,158 IU
Folate	22 mcg
Calcium	31 mg
Magnesium	8 mg
Potassium	111 mg
Phosphorus	10 mg
Iron	0.99 mg

Dill and peppercorn vinegar

MAKES 1 CUP

6 fresh dill sprigs

1 cup cider vinegar

1 tsp whole black peppercorns

Method

1 Wash and dry the dill.

2 In a saucepan over medium heat, bring the vinegar to a boil. Reduce the heat and simmer for 2 minutes. Add the dill and peppercorns, turn off the heat, and let stand for 15 minutes, until cooled.

3 Pour into a clean jar, seal, and keep in a dark place until ready to use, or refrigerate.

89 RYE

Rye provides slow-release energy because of its high fiber content. Its B vitamins do the job of unlocking this energy. The effect is good for the body and the mind.

The zinc in rye works in combination with vitamin B6 and magnesium to enable the body to produce the mood-enhancing brain chemical serotonin. Zinc is responsible for growth, too, so a breast-feeding mother's levels can be easily depleted in service of her baby's rapid growth rate. Zinc also promotes healing. An inadequate amount of this mineral can reduce milk supply by lowering prolactin levels, the hormone responsible for signaling milk production. Zinc is also responsible for transporting vitamin A to breast milk. Most babies are born with low levels of this vitamin, so they need to take it from breast milk in the first six months of life. Children with low levels show poor resistance to infection, decreased appetite, and tendencies to iron-deficiency anemia.

DID YOU KNOW?

Sourdough rye bread, found in most supermarkets, is a better alternative to yeast-risen bread for those with thrush, which may be passed from mother to baby when breast-feeding.

MAJOR NUTRIENTS PER 100 G/ABOUT ¾ CUP DARK RYE FLOUR

Calories	325
Total fat	2.22 g
Omega-6 fatty acids	958 mg
Protein	15.91 g
Carbohydrate	68.63 g
Fiber	23.8 g
Vitamin B1	0.32 mg
Vitamin B2	0.25 mg
Vitamin B3	4.27 mg
Vitamin B5	1.46 mg
Vitamin B6	0.44 mg
Vitamin A	11 IU
Magnesium	160 mg
Iron	4.97 mg
Manganese	6.06 mg
Selenium	18 mcg
Zinc	5.04 mg
Lutein/Zeaxanthin	210 mcg

- The B vitamins, zinc, and slow-release energy help the brain combat postnatal depression.
- Zinc is a crucial component both for the baby's growth and the mother's own repair mechanisms.
- Low zinc can result in a reduced milk supply and less vitamin A in breast milk, which can affect the baby's immunity and iron levels.

Practical tips:
Rye creates a dense, less fluffy bread. This helps regulate appetite because it takes longer to chew, and chewing tells the body it has received food. This can help you manage sugar cravings that occur when energy is low.

Eggs and red bell pepper on rye toast

SERVES 4   Ⓖ Ⓑ Ⓐ Ⓥ Ⓠ

2 tbsp olive oil

1 small red bell pepper, seeded and chopped

1 small red onion, very finely chopped

pinch of paprika, plus extra to garnish (optional)

4 slices dark rye bread

8 extra-large eggs

4 tbsp milk

2 tbsp butter

pepper

Method

1 Heat half of the oil in a nonstick skillet over medium–high heat, add the red bell pepper and onion, and cook, stirring frequently, for 10 minutes, or until soft. Add the paprika, stir, and set aside.

2 Preheat the broiler to high. Toast one side of the bread slices. Brush the other sides with the remaining oil, then lightly toast. Keep warm.

3 Beat the eggs with the milk and a little pepper to taste in a bowl. Melt the butter in a nonstick saucepan, add the egg mixture, and cook over medium–high heat, stirring frequently to make sure that the eggs don't stick, for 5 minutes, or until thoroughly cooked.

4 Gently stir in the red bell pepper mixture, then spoon onto the rye toasts. Sprinkle with a little extra paprika to garnish, if using, and serve immediately.

90

PSYLLIUM HUSK POWDER

Normalizing bowel movements after childbirth is a priority, and psyllium husk powder is an effective, gentle, and safe way to ensure this.

Psyllium husk powder is the ground outer shell of the psyllium seed. It is used as a stool-softening agent because the powder easily absorbs water to form a large mass in the bowel. Psyllium seeds contain 10–30 percent of a substance called mucilage, which becomes gelatinous on contact with water. This property regulates water in the bowel, bulking out stools so they can be more easily moved in cases of constipation, and drawing out water to firm up stools in cases of diarrhea. It also helps relieve the pain of passing a stool when this is likely to put pressure on sore areas or a wound.

• Safe stool-softening mucilage that regulates bowel movements post-birth.
• Regulates water in stools to reduce the incidence of both constipation and diarrhea.

Practical tips:
Psyllium husk powder is available at most health food stores. If you are breast-feeding, buy the pure powder and not one mixed with senna. Enough water must be drunk over the course of the day to ensure the psyllium doesn't cause additional blockages. Drink at least one 8 fl oz cup of fluids for every 3–5 grams of husk taken. The usual dose is 1 teaspoon (approximately 5 grams) three times per day, but start with half of that dose and build up to avoid the possibility of an initial worsening of gas or bloating. Psyllium husk powder is most effective when taken with meals.

DID YOU KNOW?

The soluble fiber content of psyllium husk powder has been found to help regulate blood sugar in people with diabetes, which makes it a particularly useful preparation for diabetic new mothers. It is safe to take while breast-feeding.

MAJOR NUTRIENTS PER 5 G/1 TSP PSYLLIUM HUSK POWDER

Calories	7
Total fat	0 g
Protein	0 g
Carbohydrate	2 g
Fiber	1.8 g
Calcium	4.32 mg
Iron	0.03 mg

Apple, carrot, and cucumber juice

SERVES 1 (A)(N)(V)(Q)

1 apple, unpeeled, cored,
    and chopped
1 carrot, peeled and chopped
½ cucumber, chopped
1 cup water
1 tsp psyllium husk powder
pieces of carrot, cucumber,
    and apple on a toothpick,
    to decorate

Method

1 Place the apple, carrot, cucumber, and water into a food processor or blender and process. Pour into a glass and stir in the psyllium husk powder.

2 Set the toothpick on top of the glass. Serve immediately.

91 SPINACH

The dark green color of spinach demonstrates its high levels of protective carotenoid antioxidants, including vitamin A, beta-carotene, lutein, and zeaxanthin.

The carotenoids that protect the plant as it photosynthesizes, or draws energy from sunlight, also protect the fatty areas of our bodies. After birth, this means the healing of damaged skin and tissues, helping bring down inflammation and creating new tissues as the womb and abdominal skin return to normal. Breast milk contains carotenoids at higher levels in the first few days of production. The reason for this is not completely understood, but it is believed to help a newborn's transition from the womb to the harsher outside world. Lutein remains high for longest, possibly to protect the baby's vulnerable eyes from exposure to light. The folate (folic acid) in spinach also supports the growth of both mother's and breastfed baby's new tissues. The vitamin K enables bone growth and, because the baby cannot make this, he or she has to rely on its presence in milk.

- Antioxidant carotenoids help heal post-birth damage.
- Supplies carotenoids for breast milk, protecting a new baby against light exposure.
- Folate supports healing and repair.
- Vitamin K is passed to the baby for steady bone development.

Practical tips:
Eating plenty of green leafy vegetables is one of the foundations of health. Vitamin C and folate are easily damaged by cooking, so lightly steaming is a more nutritious solution than boiling the leaves.

DID YOU KNOW?

Spinach contains both iron and vitamin C. The vegetable nonheme form of iron is less easily utilized than the animal heme form, and needs vitamin C to help its absorption.

MAJOR NUTRIENTS PER 100 G/3½ OZ SPINACH

Calories	23
Total fat	0.4 g
Protein	2.2 g
Carbohydrate	3.6 g
Fiber	2.2 g
Vitamin C	28 mg
Vitamin A	9,377 IU
Beta-carotene	5,626 mcg
Vitamin E	2.03 mg
Vitamin K	483 mcg
Folate	194 mcg
Calcium	99 mg
Magnesium	79 mg
Iron	2.71 mg
Lutein/Zeaxanthin	12,198 mcg

Mushroom, spinach, and rice burgers

SERVES 4–6 (G) (A)

2 tbsp brown rice

4 tbsp olive oil

3–4 garlic cloves, crushed

4 cups chopped button
    mushrooms

6 oz fresh spinach leaves
    (about 6 cups)

10 oz of canned cranberry beans,
    drained (1 cup)

1 orange bell pepper, seeded,
    peeled, and finely chopped

½ cup slivered almonds

½ cup grated Parmesan cheese

2 tbsp chopped fresh basil

1 cup fresh whole wheat
    breadcrumbs

2 tbsp whole wheat flour

1–2 beef tomatoes, thickly sliced

4–6 large portobello mushrooms

pepper

Method

1 Cook the rice in a saucepan of boiling water for 20–25 minutes, or until tender. Drain and place in a food processor.

2 Heat 1 tablespoon of the oil in a skillet. Add the garlic and button mushrooms and cook for 5 minutes. Add to the rice in the food processor.

3 Reserve a handful of the spinach. Add the remaining spinach, the beans, bell pepper, almonds, Parmesan cheese, basil, breadcrumbs, and pepper to taste to the rice mixture in the food processor and, using the pulse button, chop finely. Mix well, then shape into 4–6 equal-size burgers. Coat in the flour, then cover and let chill in the refrigerator for 1 hour.

4 Preheat the broiler to medium–high. Heat 2 tablespoons of the oil in a nonstick skillet and cook the burgers for 5–6 minutes on each side, or until golden and cooked through. Meanwhile, brush the tomato slices and portobello mushrooms with the remaining oil and broil for 6–8 minutes, turning once, until softened.

5 Place the reserved spinach on individual serving plates and top each with a mushroom. Add the burgers and tomato slices and serve immediately.

92

PLUMS

Along with berries and apples, plums rank in the top twenty foods in the ORAC table. These superfoods have the very best postnatal immune and healing potential.

The ORAC (oxygen radical absorption capacity) scale measures the antioxidant capacity of plants and identifies the foods we need to consume regularly in order to neutralize free radicals and help prevent diseases. After birth, when the body cannot afford to waste its energy on dealing with infections, these needs are at their highest. Eating plums, and other chart-topping ORAC foods, will help reduce the impact of milk production and the body's necessary healing work. Supporting your immune function in this way will also make the need for antibiotics less likely, which, if you're breast-feeding, can lead to oral thrush for your baby. Plums contain high levels of the potent antioxidant chlorogenic acid and also the soluble fiber pectin, which helps to keep the bowels healthy and toxins removed from the digestive tract.

- High antioxidant profile helps prevent inflammation and infection, helping the body to use its energy for healing and producing milk.
- Help lower the likelihood of antibiotic use by supporting immunity.
- The fiber pectin eases bowel movements and prevents the absorption of toxins.

Practical tips:
Like apples and rhubarb, plums can be stewed to make a naturally gentle laxative. The result is delicious added to muesli, oatmeal, or yogurt and will keep things moving without discomfort.

DID YOU KNOW?

Plums are naturally high in the chemical serotonin, which raises mood and can help ward off postnatal depression. Other happy foods are avocados, bananas, eggplant, pineapple, tomatoes, and walnuts.

MAJOR NUTRIENTS PER AVERAGE-SIZE PLUM

Calories	30
Total fat	trace
Protein	0.5 g
Carbohydrate	7.5 g
Fiber	0.9 g
Vitamin C	6.3 mg
Vitamin K	4.2 mcg
Potassium	104 mg
Beta-carotene	125 mcg
Lutein/Zeaxanthin	48 mcg

Spiced plum cupcakes

SERVES 4   (A) (V)

4 tbsp butter, softened, plus extra
    for greasing

¼ cup sugar

1 extra-large egg, lightly beaten

½ cup whole wheat flour

½ tsp baking powder

1 tsp ground allspice

¼ cup coarsely ground
    blanched hazelnuts

2 small plums, halved, pitted,
    and sliced

Greek-style yogurt, to serve

Method

1 Preheat the oven to 350°F. Grease four ²/₃-cup ovenproof teacups with butter.

2 Put the butter and sugar in a bowl and beat together until light and fluffy. Gradually beat in the egg. Sift in the flour, baking powder, and allspice (tipping any bran left in the sifter into the bowl) and, using a metal spoon, fold into the batter with the ground hazelnuts. Spoon the batter into the prepared teacups. Arrange the sliced plums on top of the batter.

3 Put the teacups on a baking sheet and bake in the preheated oven for 25 minutes, or until risen and firm to the touch. Serve warm or cold with Greek-style yogurt.

93

SARDINES

Obtaining complete good-quality protein from sardines and other oily fish helps recovery and mood. The omega-3 fatty acids they contain are a vital component of breast milk.

MAJOR NUTRIENTS PER 135 G/5 OZ (ABOUT 3) SARDINES

Calories	280
Total fat	16 g
Omega-3 fatty acids—EPA	1,147 mg
Omega-3 fatty acids—DHA	1,550 mg
Protein	33 g
Carbohydrate	0 g
Fiber	0 g
Vitamin B3	7 mg
Vitamin B5	0.87 mg
Vitamin B12	15 mcg
Vitamin A	302.4 IU
Vitamin D	367.2 IU
Vitamin E	2.7 mg
Magnesium	53 mg
Potassium	536 mg
Iron	3.9 mg
Zinc	1.8 mg
Selenium	71 mcg

Studies clearly show that a mother's levels of dietary omega-3 fatty acids are reflected in her breast milk. This finding refers specifically to DHA, the direct form of omega-3 found only in oily fish and incorporated into our brain cells. Many studies have linked low DHA to an increased risk of sudden infant death syndrome (SIDS), the development of attention deficit hyperactivity disorder (ADHD), schizophrenia, poor sleep patterns, asthma, eczema, and lower IQ. Low levels in mothers are associated with postnatal depression. Sardines provide the vital brain and mood-supporting combination of good-quality protein, the B vitamins, vitamins A and D, and minerals.

• Direct form of DHA, resulting in healthy breast milk and a lowered risk of ADHD, asthma, eczema, poor brain development, and mental health issues for the child.
• DHA in combination with protein, vitamins, and minerals may help prevent postnatal depression, or milder unhappy feelings.

Practical tips:

Due to possible contamination, the recommendation while breast-feeding is to eat no more than 12 oz of fish that is lower in mercury a week. However, some scientists believe that the negative effects of too little DHA far outweigh the risk from toxins. You may prefer to take a fish oil supplement, but first check with your health-care provider. Vegetarians should use a vegan marine algae source.

Sardines with Mediterranean spinach

SERVES 4   (**G**) (**B**) (**A**) (**Q**)

3 tbsp olive oil

*finely grated rind and juice
    of 1 orange*

1 small red onion, thinly sliced

1 garlic clove, very finely chopped

12 fresh thyme sprigs

*12 sardines, heads removed,
    gutted and rinsed inside and out*

chopped fresh cilantro, to garnish

Mediterranean spinach

1½ tbsp olive oil

1 onion, chopped

1 large garlic clove, crushed

2 tsp ground coriander

2 tsp ground cumin

2 lb baby leaf spinach, rinsed

½ cup pine nuts, lightly toasted

pepper

Method

1 Put the oil, orange rind and juice, onion, and garlic in a flat bowl large enough to hold all the sardines and whisk until blended. Put a thyme sprig inside each sardine, then add the fish to the marinade and use your hands to coat them.

2 Preheat the broiler to high. Line the broiler pan with foil. To make the Mediterranean spinach, heat the oil in a skillet over medium–high heat. Add the onion and cook, stirring, for 3 minutes, then add the garlic and continue to cook, stirring, until the onion is soft. Stir in the coriander and cumin and continue to cook, stirring, for a minute.

3 Add the spinach with just the water clinging to its leaves, using a wooden spoon to push it into the skillet, and add pepper to taste. Cook, stirring, for 6–8 minutes, or until the leaves are wilted. Sprinkle with the pine nuts, then cover and keep warm while you broil the sardines.

4 Arrange the sardines in the pan, brush with the marinade, and place 4 inches beneath the heat. Broil for 1½ minutes.

5 Turn the fish, then brush with more marinade and broil for 1½–2 minutes, until the fish is cooked through and the flesh flakes easily. Serve with the Mediterranean spinach.

94 ORANGES

Oranges are known to be high in healing and protective vitamin C, but they also provide an easily digested form of calcium that gives protection to postnatal bones.

MAJOR NUTRIENTS PER MEDIUM-SIZE ORANGE

Calories	65
Total fat	trace
Protein	1 g
Carbohydrate	16 g
Fiber	3.4 g
Vitamin C	64 mg
Vitamin A	298 IU
Folate	39.8 mcg
Calcium	61 mg
Potassium	238 mg
Lutein/Zeaxanthin	182 mcg

Calcium is of optimum importance during this time. First, the stocks that were used during pregnancy for the development of the baby's skeleton need to be replaced. The chances are that some of that calcium was taken from the bones and teeth and not only from the diet. The needs of breast-feeding mothers must be kept up as they are continuing to provide calcium, vitamin C, vitamin A, and folate (folic acid) for the baby's bones. Oranges contain vitamin C, needed to produce collagen, which is present in all of our body structures. Vitamin C cannot be stored in the body and should be consumed on a daily basis. After pregnancy, a lack can reveal itself in poor hair, nail, and skin quality, and bones and teeth can be affected. The antioxidants in oranges help to reduce inflammatory symptoms, such as mastitis and poor wound healing.

• Calcium is supplied to the baby in breast milk, and ensures the mother's bones and teeth stay at optimum health after pregnancy.
• Vitamin C promotes collagen for the repair of hair, skin, and nails.
• High antioxidant load helps reduce inflammation that can lead to mastitis and poor healing capacity.

Practical tips:
Whole oranges are the best way to receive the nutrients. You get more of an antioxidant and healing boost from eating a fresh orange than drinking juice, and retaining the fiber means you avoid the risk of a sugar rush.

Exotic fruit cocktail

SERVES 4 (G) (A) (V) (Q)

2 oranges
2 large passion fruit
1 pineapple
1 pomegranate
1 banana

Method

1 Cut 1 orange in half and squeeze the juice into a bowl, discarding any seeds. Using a sharp knife, cut away all the peel and pith from the second orange. Working over the bowl to catch the juice, carefully cut the orange segments between the membranes to obtain skinless segments of fruit. Discard any seeds.

2 Cut the passion fruit in half, scoop the flesh into a nylon strainer, and, using a spoon, push the pulp and juice into the bowl of orange segments. Discard the seeds.

3 Using a sharp knife, cut away all the skin from the pineapple and cut the flesh lengthwise into quarters. Cut away the central hard core. Cut the flesh into chunks and add to the orange-and-passion fruit mixture. Cover and refrigerate the fruit at this stage if you are not serving immediately.

4 Cut the pomegranate into quarters and, using your fingers or a teaspoon, remove the red seeds from the membrane. Cover and refrigerate until ready to serve.

5 Just before serving, peel and slice the banana, add to the fruit cocktail with the pomegranate seeds, and mix thoroughly. Serve immediately.

95

ROMAINE LETTUCE

The more anti-inflammatory foods that you eat, such as romaine lettuce, the greater your body's ability to soothe and heal inflamed body tissues.

Romaine lettuce contains plenty of vital folate (folic acid). This B vitamin plays a crucial role in all the body's growth and repair because it is needed to manufacture RNA and DNA proteins, our genetic materials. These tell the body how and when to provide new proteins for growth. Folate also helps the body make new red blood cells and immune system cells, for the breast-fed baby, too. The bitter taste of the leaves helps stimulate bile flow, and, therefore, digestion, so that the body gets the most nutrients from the food you eat. The digestive system may still be slower immediately after birth, but this stimulation will reduce any tendencies to have gas or constipation. The generous fiber levels in romaine also help to form easy-to-pass stools that won't aggravate a sore perineum.

- Folate enables growth and repair, and also produces red blood cells and immune cells for mother and breast-fed baby.
- Sluggish digestion post-pregnancy is stimulated by the bitter taste.
- Fiber helps to soften stools, making them less painful to pass after childbirth.

Practical tips:
Romaine, or cos, lettuce can be eaten like any salad green. If constipated or experiencing gas, eat it regularly for its water content. The larger, sturdier leaves make a good alternative to wraps if you find bread or wheat products difficult to digest.

DID YOU KNOW?

People who eat fewer than three vegetables a day, or who rarely eat green leafy vegetables, such as romaine lettuce, have been found to have inadequate levels of folic acid. The need for folic acid remains high after pregnancy for healing and breast milk supply for your baby.

MAJOR NUTRIENTS PER 100 G/ABOUT 2 CUPS ROMAINE LETTUCE

Calories	17
Total fat	0.3 g
Protein	1.2 g
Carbohydrate	3.3 g
Fiber	2.1 g
Vitamin C	24 mg
Folate	136 mcg
Calcium	33 mg
Potassium	247 mg

Lettuce, chickpea, and tomato salad

SERVES 4 (G) (A) (V) (Q)

14 oz of canned chickpeas
(garbanzo beans), drained and
rinsed (1⅔ cups)
2 ripe tomatoes, coarsely chopped
1 small red onion, thinly sliced
handful fresh basil leaves, torn
1 romaine or cos lettuce, torn
fresh crusty bread, to serve

Dressing
1 garlic clove, crushed
juice and zest of 1 lemon
3 tbsp olive oil
1 tbsp water
pepper

Method

1 To make the dressing, put all the ingredients into a small screw-top jar and shake until well blended. Taste and add more lemon juice or oil, if necessary.

2 Put the chickpeas, tomatoes, onion, and basil in a serving bowl and mix gently. Pour over the dressing and mix again. Arrange on a bed of lettuce and serve with crusty bread.

96 WATERMELON

Watermelon is high in the carotenoid lycopene, which gives it its red color. This protective nutrient is passed to the baby in breast milk.

Eating a rainbow of fruit and vegetables ensures that the full spectrum of antioxidants is made available to both mother and breast-fed baby, lowering the risk of infectious disease and inflammatory conditions, such as asthma, eczema, and mastitis. The lycopene in watermelon specifically protects fatty areas of the body, including the brain, heart, and liver. L-citrulline, an amino acid in the fruit, is converted by the body to L-arginine and helps reduce high blood pressure. This action is heightened by the potassium content of watermelon, which encourages levels to normalize in the stressful period after pregnancy. The potassium and slow-release natural sugars help take watermelon's high water content into our cells for hydration. This is a crucial health concern post-pregnancy because so much fluid is lost in birth, and especially so while breast-feeding, when the body has to produce at least an extra pint of fluid a day.

- Antioxidant carotenoid provides protection to fatty areas of the brain, heart, and liver post-birth; a breast-fed baby also benefits.
- L-citrulline and potassium help normalize high blood pressure.
- High water content, potassium, and natural sugars help hydration.

Practical tips:
Cut or juice watermelon immediately before eating to retain its vitamin C content. The antioxidant carotenoids are better absorbed with some oil present—add to a salad with an olive oil dressing, or enjoy after a meal.

DID YOU KNOW?
Vitamin C and lycopene help protect the heart from future disease risk—an important consideration when women's heart disease is on the rise, and pregnancy forces the heart to work 25 percent harder.

MAJOR NUTRIENTS PER 100 G/ABOUT ⅔ CUP WATERMELON

Calories	30
Total fat	0.15 g
Protein	0.61 g
Carbohydrate	7.55 g
Fiber	0.4 g
Vitamin C	8.1 mg
Potassium	112 mg
Lycopene	4,532 mcg
Beta-carotene	303 mcg

Fruit cocktail with granola

SERVES 4 Ⓐ Ⓥ Ⓠ

¼ cup rolled oats

1 tbsp sesame seeds

pinch of ground ginger

1 tbsp sunflower seeds

2 tsp freshly squeezed orange juice

1 tsp honey

Fruit cocktail

2 cups peeled, seeded,
*   watermelon chunks*

1 orange, peeled and divided
*   into segments*

⅓ cup freshly squeezed
*   orange juice*

1 tsp finely grated orange zest

1 tsp peeled and finely sliced
*   fresh ginger*

1 tsp honey

Method

1 Preheat the oven to 350°F.

2 To make the granola, put all the dry ingredients into a bowl, then add the orange juice and honey and mix thoroughly. Spread out on a nonstick baking sheet and bake for 7–8 minutes. Remove from the oven, break up into pieces, then return to the oven for another 7–8 minutes. Remove from the oven and break up again. Let cool on the baking sheet. The mixture will become crunchy when cool.

3 To make the fruit cocktail, put the watermelon and orange segments into a bowl. Put the orange juice and zest, ginger, and honey into a small saucepan over medium heat and bring to a boil. Pour the mixture over the fruit and let cool. Cover and chill in the refrigerator.

4 Spoon the fruit into bowls and sprinkle over the granola.

97 CRANBERRIES

After pregnancy, the kidneys and bladder can be susceptible to infection. Cranberries can help prevent these conditions, or soothe them if they have taken hold.

MAJOR NUTRIENTS PER 175 ML/¾ CUP SWEETENED CRANBERRY JUICE

Calories	108
Total fat	trace
Protein	trace
Carbohydrate	26 g
Fiber	trace
Vitamin C	60 mg
Vitamin E	trace
Lutein/Zeaxanthin	150 mcg

MAJOR NUTRIENTS PER 100 G/ABOUT 1 CUP CRANBERRIES

Calories	46
Total fat	trace
Protein	0.4 g
Carbohydrate	12.2 g
Fiber	4.6 g
Vitamin C	13 mg
Vitamin E	1.2 mcg
Lutein/Zeaxanthin	91 mcg

During the six weeks after birth, the kidneys have to work especially hard to help the body lose all the excess fluid it has been holding onto. The bladder is also recovering from being squashed by an expanded womb. These states can increase the risk of infections, including cystitis, which affects about 12 percent of women after childbirth. Cranberries contain hippuric acid and antioxidant proanthocyanidins, which have been shown to help prevent urinary tract infections (UTIs), although they will not necessarily cure them once established. Anyone who is prone to cystitis should drink a preventive glass of cranberry juice a day to ward off infection. Cranberries rank as one of the top foods on the ORAC (oxygen radical absorption capacity) antioxidant index. For this reason, they can help to heal bladder and urinary tract tissues that may have been damaged during pregnancy and birth.

- Help prevent cystitis and bladder infections in women who are susceptible or had a catheter fitted after childbirth.
- High antioxidant capacity promotes the healing of tissues that are inflamed or damaged after pregnancy and labor.

Practical tips:
Cranberries are bitter, so the juice drink is usually sweetened with sugar. For a healthier alternative, buy unsweetened cranberry juice from health food stores and mix with apple juice. One or two glasses a day should have the desired preventive effect.

Chicken and cranberry salad

SERVES 4 (G) (B) (A) (N)

1 cup dried cranberries

2 tbsp fresh apple juice or water

3 cups sugar snap peas

2 ripe avocados, halved, pitted,
   peeled, and sliced

juice of ½ lemon

4 lettuce hearts

1 bunch watercress, trimmed

3 handfuls arugula

14 oz sliced cooked chicken

½ cup chopped walnuts,
   to garnish (optional)

Dressing

2 tbsp olive oil

1 tbsp walnut oil

2 tbsp lemon juice

1 tbsp chopped fresh mixed herbs,
   such as parsley and
   lemon thyme

pepper

Method

1 Put the cranberries in a bowl. Stir in the apple juice, cover with
   plastic wrap, and let soak for 30 minutes. Meanwhile, blanch the
   sugar snap peas, refresh under cold running water, and drain.

2 Toss the avocados in the lemon juice to prevent discoloration.
   Separate the lettuce hearts and arrange on a large serving platter with
   the avocados, sugar snap peas, watercress, arugula, and chicken.

3 To make the dressing, put the first four ingredients into a small
   screw-top jar, with a little pepper to taste, and shake until combined.

4 Drain the cranberries and mix them with the dressing, then pour
   over the salad. Serve immediately, scattered with walnuts, if using.

98 FAVA BEANS

Fava beans contain L-dopa, from which we make the mood and motivation brain chemical dopamine, and so may help reduce the baby blues common after birth.

Fava beans are high in protein, magnesium, zinc, and the B vitamins, also important for production of dopamine and another mood-regulating neurotransmitter (brain chemical) serotonin. These qualities and the fiber and slow-release carbohydrates that help stop highs and lows of energy and mood are another factor to help reduce the likelihood of postnatal depression. High magnesium levels help to soothe the nervous system and ward off anxiety in your new situation, also helping you sleep when you get the chance. The B vitamins, folate (folic acid), choline, and zinc help the mechanisms that promote healing after childbirth.

- Help your body produce the mood neurotransmitters dopamine and serotonin to reduce the likelihood of postnatal depression.
- Slow-release food for sustained mood and energy levels.
- Magnesium helps keep you calm and able to sleep.
- The B vitamins, folate (folic acid), choline, and zinc all work to promote optimal healing after labor.

Practical tips:
Fava beans must be cooked to break down alkaloids that can be harmful. They are prevalent in Greek and Mediterranean cuisine and can be used as well as chickpeas (garbanzo beans) in falafel. They are Egypt's national food, made into *ful medames*, a type of dip. Fava beans are incredibly versatile, and can be used as any bean, added to soups, stews, salads, and dips.

DID YOU KNOW?

Legumes, such as fava beans, offer a good alternative to starchy carbohydrates, such as bread, pasta, and potatoes, when you require a lot of energy post-birth. They contain more protein and a variety of nutrients for your recovery phase.

MAJOR NUTRIENTS PER 100 G/ABOUT ⅔ CUP FAVA BEANS, RAW

Calories	341
Total fat	1.53 g
Protein	26.12 g
Carbohydrate	58.29 g
Vitamin B3	1.54 mg
Vitamin B5	1.59 mg
Folate	557 mcg
Choline	95.2 mg
Calcium	103 mg
Magnesium	192 mg
Potassium	1,062 mg
Iron	6.7 mg
Selenium	8.2 mcg

Spring stew

SERVES 4 Ⓐ Ⓠ

2 tbsp olive oil

4–8 pearl onions, halved

2 celery stalks, cut into
    ¼-inch slices

8 oz baby carrots, scrubbed and
    halved, if large

8 new potatoes, scrubbed and
    halved or quartered, if large

5 cups vegetable stock

14 oz of canned cannellini beans,
    drained and rinsed (1½ cups)

1 fresh bouquet garni

6 baby corn

¾ cup frozen or shelled fresh fava
    beans, thawed if frozen

½–1 savoy or green cabbage,
    about 8 oz

1½ tbsp cornstarch

2 tbsp cold water

salt and pepper

½ cup grated Parmesan or sharp
    cheddar cheese, to serve

Method

1 Heat the oil in a large, heavy-bottom saucepan, with a tight-fitting
   lid, and cook the vegetables, stirring frequently, for 5 minutes,
   or until softened.

2 Add the stock, beans, and bouquet garni, then bring to a boil.
   Reduce the heat, cover, and simmer for 12 minutes.

3 Add the baby corn and fava beans and season to taste with salt
   and pepper. Simmer for another 3 minutes. Meanwhile, discard the
   outer leaves and hard central core from the cabbage and shred the
   leaves. Add to the saucepan and simmer for another 3–5 minutes,
   or until all the vegetables are tender.

4 Blend the cornstarch with the water, stir into the saucepan, and
   cook, stirring, for 4–6 minutes, or until the liquid has thickened.
   Serve the cheese separately, for stirring into the stew.

SAVOY CABBAGE

99

Cabbage and other brassicas are an important immune-supporting part of any diet, but especially when the body's resources are low after childbirth.

Brassica (cabbage family) vegetables contain detoxifying glucosinolate chemicals that help the body regulate hormonal changes after birth. Cabbage also contains significant levels of the amino acid glutamine, which keeps the digestive tract healthy, supports muscle strength to help the body repair and cope, and has detoxifying and anti-inflammatory actions. Cabbage and other green leaves provide vitamin C and folate (folic acid), which we need to replenish daily because it is not easily stored in the body and is crucial for growth, wound repair, muscle building, energy production, and brain and heart health. A mother who is breast-feeding needs to be particularly vigilant about her intake of these nutrients because she is also providing them to her baby. A daily intake is necessary to avoid deficiency symptoms.

- Glucosinolates aid hormonal balance and immune support.
- The amino acid glutamine promotes repair, supports muscle strength, reduces soreness, and boosts digestive health.
- Provides essential vitamin C and folate for all growth and repair.

Practical tips:
Cabbage has been thought to cause gas in breast-fed babies, but gas from the mother's intestines does not pass into breast milk, so any problems in the baby are more likely caused by an immature digestive system and swallowing air. Savoy cabbage relieves sore and engorged breasts in the early stages of breast-feeding; put a refrigerated leaf in each bra cup for simple and effective relief.

DID YOU KNOW?

Breast-fed babies develop a taste for the foods their mothers eat, because the flavors pass into breast milk. A child is more likely to eat her greens if her mother did while breast-feeding.

MAJOR NUTRIENTS PER 100 G/ABOUT 1 CUP SAVOY CABBAGE

Calories	27
Total fat	trace
Protein	2 g
Carbohydrate	6.1 g
Fiber	3.1 g
Vitamin C	31 mg
Vitamin A	1,000 IU
Vitamin K	68.8 mcg
Folate	80 mcg
Calcium	35 mg
Magnesium	28 mg
Potassium	230 mg
Iron	0.7 mg
Manganese	0.2 mg
Selenium	0.9 mcg
Beta-carotene	600 mcg

Traditional bean and cabbage soup

SERVES 6 (G) (A) (V)

1 cup dried cannellini beans,
    soaked overnight
3 tbsp olive oil
2 red onions, coarsely chopped
4 carrots, peeled and sliced
4 celery stalks, coarsely chopped
4 garlic cloves, coarsely chopped
2½ cups vegetable stock
14 oz of canned chopped
    tomatoes (1¾ cups)
2 tbsp chopped fresh flat-leaf
    parsley
1 lb savoy cabbage, finely sliced
    (about 7 cups)
pepper
extra virgin olive oil, to serve

Method

1 Drain the beans and put in a large saucepan. Cover with fresh cold water and bring to a boil, skimming off any foam that rises to the surface with a slotted spoon. Reduce the heat and simmer, uncovered, for 1–1½ hours, until tender, filling up with more water, if required.

2 Meanwhile, heat the olive oil in a large saucepan, add the onions, carrots, and celery, and cook over medium heat, stirring frequently, for 10–15 minutes, until soft. Add the garlic and cook, stirring, for 1–2 minutes.

3 Drain the beans and add half to the vegetable mixture. Pour in most of the stock, add the tomatoes and parsley, and season well with pepper. Bring to a simmer and cook, uncovered and stirring occasionally, for 30 minutes. Add the savoy cabbage and cook, stirring occasionally, for an additional 15 minutes.

4 Put the remaining beans in a food processor or blender with some of the reserved cooking water and process until smooth. Add to the soup. The soup should be thick, but add more of the stock to thin, if necessary. Continue to cook until heated through. Serve hot with a drizzle of extra virgin olive oil.

100 MELON

The antioxidants in melon, which contain high levels of vitamin C, vitamin A, and beta-carotene, promote healing and repair all over the body.

The high vitamin C content of melon helps fight off viruses and bacteria in the watery areas between and inside cells, increasing immune white cell production. This process is crucial in the fight against infection and illness at a time when the body may have large wounds to heal and tissues vulnerable to invasion. The vitamin C also reactivates the water-soluble vitamin E so that it can be used again. The vitamin A and beta-carotene present in melon have been shown particularly to help lung development; good levels in breast milk help the baby take on oxygen and grow. This is especially important if the baby was born prematurely, when the lungs may not be completely developed. These nutrients also help vision and protect the baby's eyes from light after being in the womb. Beta-carotene is taken into breast milk in especially high levels immediately after birth.

- Vitamin C actively prevents viral and bacterial infection.
- Vitamin C recycles healing vitamin E.
- Vitamin A and beta-carotene help ensure the correct levels in breast milk for the baby's lung and eye development.

Practical tips:
Choose ripe melons—their beta-carotene levels are at their highest when they are at their most orange. They are also particularly sweet at this time. Add melon to other fruits to make a fruit salad, but remember that it starts to lose its vitamin C as soon as it is cut.

DID YOU KNOW?

As melon, and other fruits and vegetables ripen, the green chlorophyll converts to potent antioxidants called NCCs (nonfluorescing chlorophyll catabolytes).

MAJOR NUTRIENTS PER MEDIUM-SIZE CANTALOUPE MELON WEDGE

Calories	35
Total fat	trace
Protein	0.86 g
Carbohydrate	8.32 g
Fiber	0.9 g
Vitamin C	37.4 mg
Vitamin A	3,450 IU
Vitamin E	0.1 mg
Potassium	272 mg
Beta-carotene	2,060 mcg

Melon and strawberry crunch

SERVES 4   (G) (A) (V) (Q)

¼ cup oats

¼ cup oat bran

2 tbsp slivered almonds

¼ cup finely chopped plumped
   dried apricots

½ melon, such as galia,
   canteloupe, or honeydew,
   seeded, peeled, and cut into
   bite-size pieces

8 oz strawberries,
   halved if large

⅔ cup plain yogurt with live
   cultures or milk, to serve
   (optional)

Method

1   Put the rolled oats and oat bran in a bowl and stir in the almonds
   and dried apricots.

2   Divide the mixture among 4 individual bowls, then top with the
   melon and strawberries. Pour the yogurt or milk over, if using.

INDEX